my **revision** notes

AQA GCSE

PE

Kirk Bizley

HODDER
EDUCATION
AN HACHETTE UK COMPANY

Dedication

To my dearest wife Louise for her never-wavering support, and grandchild number eight, Harlowe, who was born while I was writing this!

Acknowledgements

The publishers and author would like to thank Simon Scarborough and Richard Lewis for their contributions.

Photo credits

Cover © Elena Baryshkina – Fotolia; **p.7** © Serge Mouraret/Demotix/Press Association Images; **p.8** © Alex Livesey/Getty Images; **p.10** l © Junko Kimura/Getty Images, c © Bruno Fahy/Belga/Press Association Images, r © David Davies/PA Archive/Press Association Images; **p.14** © Lee Warren/Gallo Images/Getty Images; **p.26** © Severin Schweiger/Cultura/Getty Images; **p.33** © huaxiadragon – Fotolia; **p.34** © Lensi Photography/ Demotix/Press Association Images; **p.37** © Kirk Bizley; **p.42** © Crown Copyright; **p.47** © Evan R. Sanders/ AP/Press Association Images; **p.48** © Ian Waldie/Getty Images; **p.50** © John Walton/EMPICS Sport/ Press Association Images; **p.52** © marc macdonald/Alamy; **p.54** © Sport England; **p.64** © Kevin Quigley/Associated Newspapers/Rex Features; **p.68** © Luca Bruno/AP/Press Association Images; **p.72** © Tom Dulat/Getty Images.

Orders: please contact Bookpoint Ltd, 130 Milton Park, Abingdon, Oxon OX14 4SB. Telephone: +44 (0)1235 827720. Fax: +44 (0)1235 400454. Lines are open 9.00a.m.–5.00p.m., Monday to Saturday, with a 24-hour message answering service. Visit our website at www.hoddereducation.co.uk.

© Kirk Bizley 2014
First published in 2014 by
Hodder Education,
an Hachette UK company
Carmelite House, 50 Victoria Embankment,
London EC4Y 0DZ

Impression number 10 9 8 7 6 5 4 3
Year 2018 2017 2016

Typeset in Cronos Pro by Datapage (India) Pvt. Ltd.
Artwork by Datapage
Printed and bound in India
A catalogue record for this title is available from the British Library
ISBN 978 1471 806513

Get the most from this book

This book will help you revise for the Short Course Award (Unit 1), the Full Course Award (Unit 3) and the Double Award (Units 3 and 5). You can use the contents list on pages 2 and 3 to plan your revision, topic by topic. Tick each box when you have:

1 revised and understood a topic

2 tested yourself.

You can also keep track of your revision by ticking off each topic heading through the book. You may find it helpful to add your own notes as you work through each topic. You can check your answers to the Check your understanding questions at the back of the book.

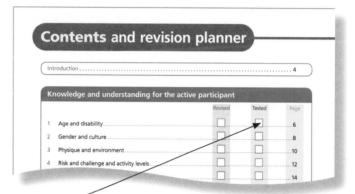

Tick to track your own progress

Exam tips

Throughout the book there are exam tips that explain how you can boost your final grade.

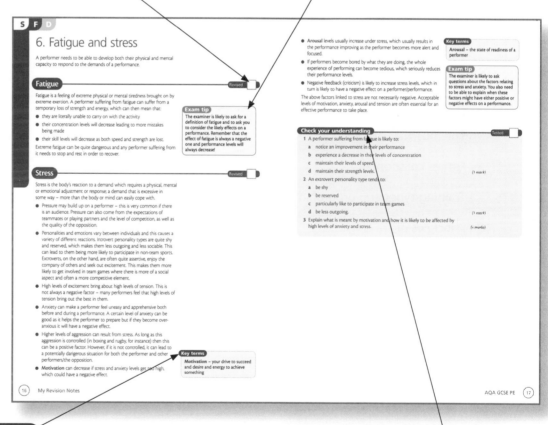

Key terms

Key terms are highlighted the first time they appear, with an explanation nearby in the margin.

Check your understanding

Use these questions at the end of each section to make sure that you have understood every topic.

Contents and revision planner

Knowledge and understanding for the active participant

Introduction

This book covers all of the content you will need to know for the three examinations which are included in the AQA PE GCSE. It is indicated within each topic whether the content is for the Double Course Award (D), Full Course Award (F) or Short Course Award (S), or for a combination of the examinations (DFS, DF or D).

There is no content which only applies to the Short Course Award, and the Double Course Award content includes *all of the* Full Course Award content too. Topic 32 covers all of the additional content which has to be covered for the Double Award only.

The three examination papers   Revised ☐

The three examination papers follow much the same format but details are as follows:

Short Course Award

- Total for the paper = 40 marks.
- Time allowed = 45 minutes.
- Section A – Part 1 = 5 multiple choice questions (5 marks).
- Section A – Part 2 = short answer questions (15 marks).
- Section B – questions based on the preliminary material – the scenario (20 marks).
- One question in Section B must be written in continuous prose and is also assessed against criteria judging your ability to:
  - use good English
  - organise information clearly
  - use specialist vocabulary where appropriate.

Full Course Award

- Total for the paper = 80 marks.
- Time allowed = 1 hour 30 minutes.
- Section A – Part 1 = 10 multiple choice questions (10 marks).
- Section A – Part 2 = short answer questions (30 marks).
- Section B – questions based on the preliminary material – the scenario (40 marks).

- Two questions in Section B must be written in continuous prose and are also assessed against criteria judging your ability to:
  - use good English
  - organise information clearly
  - use specialist vocabulary where appropriate.

Double Award

- Total for the paper = 70 marks.
- Time allowed = 1 hour 30 minutes.
- Section A – Short answer questions (49 marks).
- Section B – questions based on the preliminary material – the *additional* Double Award scenario (21 marks).
- Two questions in Section B must be written in continuous prose and are also assessed against criteria judging your ability to:
  - use good English
  - organise information clearly
  - use specialist vocabulary where appropriate.

The main differences between the Full Course and Double Award are that the Double Award does not have a multiple choice section and it has a separate and different scenario to the Full Award one.

Also, be aware that if you are entered for the Double Award you will be taking two examination papers on two different dates as you have to sit the Full Course Award paper too!

All of the following apply to all three of the examinations:

● You must answer in black pen and write your answers *within* the margins. The reason for this is that all pages of the papers have bar codes on them. These are scanned at the examination board and sent out to examiners for them to mark electronically. Black ink shows up clearly and anything written outside of the margin does not get picked up by the scanning machine!

● Write clearly and legibly. The examiner has to be able to read what you have written.

● Read the whole paper through carefully before you start. Consider this to be your 'warm-up' as it will give you time to clear your thoughts and get a general 'feel' for the paper overall.

● You do not have to answer the questions in the order they are written. Answering those you are most confident about first should get you off to a good start.

● Read the question very carefully before starting to answer it. Make sure that you are answering the question that was asked and that you have answered in full. Be sure to give examples if they are asked for. This is very common, especially in the short answer questions.

● Look out for the questions which require the use of good English – this will be clearly indicated on the question. You cannot use bullet points to answer these questions as they must be written in continuous prose.

● Check all of your answers very carefully when you have finished. This is your 'cool-down' when you make sure that you have answered correctly, fully and clearly. Sometimes, just adding one more additional word to your answer can make the difference between it being seen as 'too vague' (the most common reason given by marking examiners for not giving marks) and being detailed and specific enough to get the full marks possible.

● Make use of all of the time you have been given – there is enough time for you to answer all of the questions (and it is crucial that all are answered) so if you have additional time at the end use this for the checking process and do it thoroughly.

General tips

You need to revise everything thoroughly. There is a lot of content and it is not possible for it all to be examined in one exam. This means that you will revise a lot of content which you will not be asked a question on. However, the examiner can ask a question on any of the content so you must be prepared for any topic, or topics, to come up.

The examination is usually fairly early on in the series of examinations (usually around the second or third week in May) so you have to time your revision schedule carefully. Putting together a revision schedule just after Easter would be a good idea. This book is designed to take you through all of the content in the order it appears in the exam specification. Everything that could be asked is included and you do not need to know any additional topics. Revising too much content is as bad as revising too little.

Finally, good luck in all your exams!

1. Age and disability

Age

Age is a factor over which you have no control. It is also a **physiological factor**: there are various physical effects which ageing has on the body. These effects can then influence levels of participation in physical activities.

- Very young children cannot cope with difficult tasks, which can affect their ability to learn and practise. This is why some sports are not introduced until children are older.
- Flexibility decreases with age and therefore makes some activities, such as gymnastics, more difficult as you get older.
- Oxygen capacity and reaction time decrease as you get older.
- Injury and disease become more common as you get older, bones can become more brittle and recovery times are longer.
- Skill levels start to increase as you get into your teens and twenties but may then start to decline as you get older.
- Strength, like skill, starts to increase as you get older, peaking in the twenties and thirties but then decreasing as you enter your forties.

Age divisions

Because age can be such a deciding factor for the majority of sports, especially for younger people, competition is usually divided up into set categories. In school this is usually organised as year groups but sports and governing bodies also organise competitions into particular age groups such as under fourteens, under sixteens and under eighteens. This still allows a particularly gifted young performer to take part in a category above their age but does not allow for an older performer to drop down an age category.

> **Key term**
>
> **Physiological factor** – one that affects your living body and therefore affects you physically

> **Exam tip**
>
> Remember that the particular age of a participant can be an advantage *or* a disadvantage – often depending upon the type of activity undertaken.

Some activities clearly get more difficult as you get older!

> **Exam tip**
>
> It is important to know why age divisions are put in place – these all link to the physiological factors identified in this topic.

Disability

Disability can be physical or mental. It can also be permanent or temporary. Physical activities are now organised very efficiently to take into account the factor of disability. For example:

- Adapted activities – there is a huge range of ways in which activities are adapted to allow disabled people to participate; **for example, wheelchair rugby, which has specific rules relating to how the wheelchairs themselves can be used in physical contact.**
- Adapted equipment – such as the footballs used by blind footballers that have ball bearings inside the ball, which the players can hear as the ball moves.

- Disability classifications – these ensure that disabled competitors are able to compete with others who have the same, or a very similar, disability, so making the competition fairer.

- Provision for the disabled – this includes designated wider parking bays in car parks, ramp access for wheelchairs, disabled lifts, automatic doors, special changing areas and toilets, wider corridors, etc.

Disabled sports are now recognised as sports in their own right and there is much less discrimination against disabled participants than there used to be.

↑ Competitors in the 2013 IPC Athletics World Championships held in Lyon, France

Exam tip

The examiner may ask how the disabled are catered for as particular types of participants and also how both sports and competitions are organised for them.

Check your understanding   Tested

1 Which of the following is *not* likely to decrease as you get older?

   a Strength

   b Oxygen capacity

   c Learning ability

   d Reaction time   *(1 mark)*

2 Explain why age divisions are commonly used in competitive sport and give an example.   *(4 marks)*

3 Give four ways that disability might affect participation in physical activities.   *(4 marks)*

2. Gender and culture

Gender

The anatomical differences between males and females means that there are differences in their physical capabilities. Allowances are made for this: for example, in GCSE PE controlled assessment (practical assessment), boys are always assessed against other boys and girls against the girls, with both being assessed against the set criteria.

Gender differences

● The body shapes, physiques and sizes (and therefore **metabolism**) of men and women are generally different. Women tend to be smaller and have a flatter, broader pelvis and smaller heart and lungs.

● Women have more body fat – up to 30 per cent more.

● On average, women have two-thirds the strength of men, with less total muscle mass. This clearly disadvantages women in strength-based events.

● Levels of flexibility tend to be greater in females, often helped by their having less muscle mass.

● Boys tend to overtake girls in terms of height, weight and strength from about the age of eleven. This is one of the reasons why single-sex sport tends to be practised from this age onwards.

● Women may find their performance is affected when they are having their period; men tend to be less affected by hormonal changes.

> **Key term**
>
> **Metabolism** – the biochemical processes that happen in the body and keep us alive

Perceived differences

The physical differences related to gender are clear. However, this does not mean that either gender is particularly advantaged or disadvantaged: both may have advantages and disadvantages in all sports. At one time some sports were only considered to be suitable for one sex (netball for women and football for men, for example) but this is not the case now. Women were discriminated against in the past and not allowed to take part in some events and activities but there are equal opportunities in place now.

↑ **Zara Philips taking part in the 2012 Olympics – men and women compete on equal terms in horse-riding events as there are no perceived advantages or disadvantages relating to gender in these events**

> **Exam tip**
>
> The examiner may ask how gender can affect participation and performance in physical activity, so it is important to be aware of all the factors that relate to this.

Some **cultures** may encourage greater levels of participation in sport than others, especially in relation to gender and religion. In certain cultures the role of women is perceived as being in the home, which can limit participation.

Key term

Culture – the ideas, customs and social behaviour of a particular people or society

Gender

People's cultural attitudes change over time. **For example, until quite recently there was a lot of opposition to women's boxing in the UK.** Some religions have single-sex rules that can prevent women from taking part in mixed-sex sport activities.

Religion

Many religions also have particular dress codes which particularly relate to what women are required to wear. This applies to swimming, where some modesty rules forbid the wearing of swimming costumes if men are present.

Religious dress codes can also involve the head and hair. For instance, the Sikh religion requires that men wear a turban (sometimes a smaller version of the turban, called a patka). This could potentially cause problems in some activities; **for example, if a safety helmet was also required or in swimming activities**.

Some religions also have dietary guidelines that could affect training and competition; **for example, fasting during Ramadan in Islam**. Guidelines may also be in place that forbid taking part on certain days. **For example, in Judaism and in Christianity there are rules about keeping one day a week as a special day for prayer and family**.

Exam tip

Make sure you know how some religions encourage greater participation in sport than others. It is important to know about cultural beliefs that can restrict participation in different ways, and the reasons why these can restrict participation.

Check your understanding ————————————————————————————— Tested

1 Which one of the following shows the effects of gender on participation in physical activity?

   a   Females have lower levels of concentration than males in physical activities.

   b   Males feel more pain than females in physical activities.

   c   Males are generally stronger than females.

   d   Females are less likely to show high skill levels in physical activities. *(1 mark)*

2 Explain why the majority of sports become single sex as males and females get older. *(4 marks)*

3 Describe the ways in which the culture of a particular society might influence certain levels of participation in physical activities. *(4 marks)*

3. Physique and environment

Physique

An individual's physique is very closely linked to their body type or **somatotype**. There are three specific categories of somatotype:

1 **Endomorph** – this body type typically has wide hips and narrow shoulders. This type tends to have a rounded appearance, has trouble losing weight, but can gain muscle. They are most suited to specific sports that do not require high levels of speed or mobility, due to their additional weight.

2 **Mesomorph** – this body type typically has wide shoulders and narrow hips. They tend to have a muscular, athletic build with little body fat and are able to gain muscle relatively easily. They are therefore suited to specific sports requiring speed, strength and power.

3 **Ectomorph** – this body type typically has narrow shoulders and narrow hips. They tend to be tall and thin with a delicate build and are lightly muscled. They are therefore suited to endurance-type events.

These are descriptions of extreme endomorphs, mesomorphs and ectomorphs, which are not very common. Most individuals are a combination of the three types.

An individual's body type can make them more or less suited to a particular sporting activity or a particular playing position or role within a sport.

> **Key term**
>
> **Somatotype** – body type (endomorph, mesomorph or ectomorph.)

> **Exam tip**
>
> Make sure you know reasons why a particular body type might make a person particularly suited to a particular sport or playing position/role.

↑ Endomorph: Wide hips and narrow shoulders

↑ Mesomorph: Wide shoulders and narrow hips

↑ Ectomorph: Narrow shoulders and narrow hips

Environment

The environment is made up of lots of different factors, which can affect participation on their own or combine together in different ways:

- **Weather** – too wet, too hot, too windy, too sunny, too foggy or misty or even too dark: any of these conditions could affect the participant and their performance.

- **Pollution** – for example, severe air pollution could affect both training and participation as it can be a real health risk for participants in physical activity.

- **Altitude** (the height of an area above sea level) – this can have a positive or negative effect. Performers who regularly train at high altitude can gain the advantage of increasing the oxygen-carrying capacity of the blood. However, an individual not used to competing at high altitude is likely to find that the initial experience is uncomfortable and leaves them quite breathless.

- **Humidity** – this relates to the amount of water vapour which is present in the air. High humidity levels can result in performers overheating and suffering from **dehydration**. This is because high humidity stops sweat evaporating, which is one important way that the body cools itself down.

- **Access** – the environment in which a facility is located may make access either easier or more difficult. **For example, some rural areas may not have very good public transport, making it hard for people to get to facilities if they don't have a car**.

- **Terrain** – this relates to the natural features of an area. Some terrain (such as hilly or even mountainous) might be difficult to access but be well suited to a particular activity such as climbing, cycling or skiing.

> **Key term**
>
> **Dehydration** – the loss of water from the body

> **Exam tip**
>
> Exam questions often ask how the environment is going to either affect the participant and/or their performance. It would be good to know a suitable example to explain your answer.

Check your understanding

Tested

1 An endomorph:

   a has wide hips

   b has wide shoulders

   c has narrow hips

   d is suited to speed and mobility activities. *(1 mark)*

2 Which of these activities would an ectomorph be best suited to take part in?

   a Weightlifting

   b Swimming

   c Long-distance running

   d High jump *(1 mark)*

3 Describe the ways in which the weather might affect an individual's participation in a particular physical activity. *(4 marks)*

AQA GCSE PE 11

4. Risk and challenge and activity levels

Risk and challenge
Revised

One of the main reasons why individuals decide to participate in physical activities is because they like the challenge it offers. Many people also like to have an element of acceptable risk present as well. There are two main areas related to this.

Risk assessment

This involves making sure that any potential dangers or hazards are identified before any physical activity gets underway. The environment (see page 11) has to be considered very carefully to make sure that the challenge can be faced safely and acceptably. **For example, a wet or slippery surface might mean that it would not be safe to continue with certain types of activities.**

Risk control

Risk control is about making sure that an activity is carried out as safely as possible. Risk control includes the following:

- Making sure that the rules and regulations of the activity are followed. Safety equipment may have to be worn or used and this equipment needs to be in good order and repair. General rules such as not wearing any items of jewellery should also be in place.

- Making sure that the organisers, administrators and officials are fully qualified and knowledgeable about the activity they are running.

- Making sure that safeguards are in place. This can include monitoring where different groups are (important for activities where different groups might be in different places) and making sure that the necessary first aid and emergency procedures are in place.

> **Exam tip**
>
> Make sure you know about the safeguards which are put in place to allow participation in challenging activities to take place safely.

Activity levels
Revised

Different individuals have different needs and this particularly applies to activity levels. Age is a very important factor relating to this (see topic 1), as increasing levels of activity also mean an increase in the level of demand upon the body.

Different activities put different demands upon the individual taking part.

Recreative-type activities

These activities tend not to be particularly physically demanding as they do not require a great deal of training or preparation. For example, many older participants take part in activities such as bowls, which involve only gentle **exercise**.

> **Key term**
>
> **Exercise** – activity that requires physical or mental exertion, especially when performed to develop or maintain fitness

Competitive-type activities

To take part in these type of activities performers usually need to train and regularly practise with much higher activity levels. Also, if an individual is performing at a high level, such as county or even national or international, then they have to devote a lot of time to meet the demands of their sport.

Socio-economic factors

These are factors combining two elements:

● The amount of income an individual has

● The status they have in society

Someone who is better off financially may have a greater range of opportunities available to them. Some activities are quite expensive in terms of equipment, facilities and access and so these will not necessarily be freely available for all individuals to participate in.

Also, sports that demand a lot of practice time (for example those with high levels of activity) may not be accessible to people who cannot afford much leisure time.

Activity level effects

The level at which an individual performs also has an effect. High levels of activity can bring benefits in terms of higher levels of fitness and health and also advantages, such as enjoyment and social interaction. Low levels of activity are unlikely to have the same level of positive effects (although the risk of injury may be lower).

> **Exam tip**
>
> You should be able to compare and contrast the different demands which would be made from different activity levels: such as the extremes which might exist between recreative and competitive activities.

Check your understanding   Tested ☐

1 Which one of the following would be a good example of personal protective equipment to reduce the risk of injury if participating in a physical activity?

   a A gum shield in hockey

   b A post protector in rugby

   c A crash barrier for crowd control

   d Well fitting training shoes   (1 mark)

2 Describe ways in which you might reduce the potential risks in outdoor adventurous activities.   (5 marks)

3 Explain how socio-economic factors can affect the level of activity people can commit to.   (4 marks)

5. Training

The amount of training which an individual carries out is a matter of personal choice but it can also be affected by other factors. It is important to remember that the more training someone does, the better their performance is likely to be. Higher levels of training equal greater chances of success!

Available time

Different levels of performers often have different amounts of time available to them for training. An **amateur** performer will not have as much time available as a **professional** performer.

Top-level performers would be likely to train on some aspect relating to their activity (perhaps linked to fitness, conditioning or skill acquisition) every day, often for several hours at a time. They would need to have training facilities available to them for this.

The demands for this training can also be affected by the competitive year or timetable associated with a particular activity. **For example, footballers have a playing season when they need to be ready for every competitive game, as well as an off-season (sometimes known as post-season) when they have period of recovery and then preparation for the next cycle of play.**

In many activities there are expectations that professionals either play, or are available, all year round. **For example, many professional cricketers play different seasons in different countries so they have to train constantly.**

Key terms

Amateur – someone who takes part in sport, or an activity, as a pastime or hobby rather than for financial gain

Professional – someone who takes part in sport, or an activity, as a means of earning their livelihood. They are paid to do it as a full-time job

↑ **Kevin Pietersen bats for the Delhi Daredevils as they play the Kolkata Knight Riders**

Available funding

One of the main factors linked to being able to train is whether or not funding is available to pay for it. Funding has to cover the cost of the time performers spend training, as well as other costs such as the facilities and equipment, and possibly a personal trainer.

- **Funding streams** – this is any form of funding that a performer is able to obtain. It might be as basic as a local authority giving them free access to a swimming pool for training sessions or even a small grant towards their training costs. The biggest single funding stream available is from the National Lottery. This gives a large percentage of its profits to governing bodies, which distribute these funds to individual performers in order to allow them to train regularly for major international events such as the Olympic Games. This is still one of the main forms of funding available for amateur performers.

- **Sponsorship** – this is where performers receive help from sponsors in the form of money to pay for training, free training access or equipment. There are differences between the levels of sponsorship available for different types of performers. Professionals tend to get higher levels of sponsorship because they have a higher profile than amateurs. Because more people know about them, they are better for advertising a sponsor's products or services.

> **Exam tip**
> You need to know about the ways in which levels of training are linked to levels of success. You also need to know about the ways available to performers to fund their training to allow them to spend enough time on it.

Check your understanding

1 A professional sportsperson is someone who:

   a takes part in sport as a pastime

   b performs their sport as a hobby

   c takes part for fun

   d gets paid for taking part. *(1 mark)*

2 An example of sponsorship would be:

   a a grant from a local council

   b a money gift from a local business

   c National Lottery funding

   d free training equipment provided by a major manufacturing company. *(1 mark)*

3 Give two examples of funding that amateur performers may be able to access. *(4 marks)*

6. Fatigue and stress

A performer needs to be able to develop both their physical and mental capacity to respond to the demands of a performance.

Fatigue

Fatigue is a feeling of extreme physical or mental tiredness brought on by extreme exertion. A performer suffering from fatigue can suffer from a temporary loss of strength and energy, which can then mean that:

- they are literally unable to carry on with the activity
- their concentration levels will decrease leading to more mistakes being made
- their skill levels will decrease as both speed and strength are lost.

Extreme fatigue can be quite dangerous and any performer suffering from it needs to stop and rest in order to recover.

> **Exam tip**
>
> The examiner is likely to ask for a definition of fatigue and to ask you to consider the likely effects on a performance. Remember that the effect of fatigue is always a negative one and performance levels will always decrease!

Stress

Stress is the body's reaction to a demand which requires a physical, mental or emotional adjustment or response; a demand that is excessive in some way – more than the body or mind can easily cope with.

- Pressure may build up on a performer – this is very common if there is an audience. Pressure can also come from the expectations of teammates or playing partners and the level of competition, as well as the quality of the opposition.

- Personalities and emotions vary between individuals and this causes a variety of different reactions. Introvert personality types are quite shy and reserved, which makes them less outgoing and less sociable. This can lead to them being more likely to participate in non-team sports. Extroverts, on the other hand, are often quite assertive, enjoy the company of others and seek out excitement. This makes them more likely to get involved in team games where there is more of a social aspect and often a more competitive element.

- High levels of excitement bring about high levels of tension. This is not always a negative factor – many performers feel that high levels of tension bring out the best in them.

- Anxiety can make a performer feel uneasy and apprehensive both before and during a performance. A certain level of anxiety can be good as it helps the performer to prepare but if they become over-anxious it will have a negative effect.

- Higher levels of aggression can result from stress. As long as this aggression is controlled (in boxing and rugby, for instance) then this can be a positive factor. However, if it is not controlled, it can lead to a potentially dangerous situation for both the performer and other performers/the opposition.

- **Motivation** can decrease if stress and anxiety levels get too high, which could have a negative effect.

> **Key term**
>
> **Motivation** – your drive to succeed and desire and energy to achieve something

- **Arousal** levels usually increase under stress, which usually results in the performance improving as the performer becomes more alert and focused.

- If performers become bored by what they are doing, the whole experience of performing can become tedious, which seriously reduces their performance levels.

- Negative feedback (criticism) is likely to increase stress levels, which in turn is likely to have a negative effect on a performer/performance.

The above factors linked to stress are not necessarily negative. Acceptable levels of motivation, anxiety, arousal and tension are often essential for an effective performance to take place.

Check your understanding
Tested

1 A performer suffering from fatigue is likely to:

  a   notice an improvement in their performance

  b   experience a decrease in their levels of concentration

  c   maintain their levels of speed

  d   maintain their strength levels.   (1 mark)

2 An extrovert personality type tends to:

  a   be shy

  b   be reserved

  c   particularly like to participate in team games

  d   be less outgoing.   (1 mark)

3 Explain what is meant by motivation and how it is likely to be affected by high levels of anxiety and stress.   (4 marks)

7. Injury and safe practice

All possible precautions need to be taken to ensure that injuries do not occur.

Precautions

Revised ☐

The specific categories which need to be covered are as follows:

1 **Correct technique** – in any physical activity it is essential that correct techniques are used; this is particularly the case in many invasion games where some level of physical contact is either allowed or probable. **For example, in rugby, full contact tackling is allowed and incorrect techniques can lead to a serious injury. This is also true of football.**

2 **Safe practice** – this means ensuring that general rules (such as the correct way to lift, carry and place equipment) are adhered to; **for example, making sure that jewellery is not worn.**

3 **Clothing** – this needs to be appropriate for the activity being carried out. Each activity has its own acceptable clothing expectations and requirements. **For example, light and loose clothing might be appropriate for dance but loose clothing is not appropriate for trampolining.**

4 **Equipment** – there are two main categories:
   a Personal equipment – items of equipment that a performer might need, such as gum shields, shin pads, face mask/batting helmet, batting/goal-keepers' gloves, trampoline shoes, studded boots/athletic spikes, etc. There may also be larger personal equipment to consider, such as bats/hockey sticks, javelins, climbing ropes and so on.
   b General activity-specific equipment – this includes post protectors, trampolines and frame protectors, long-jump pits (condition and the use of rakes), landing mats (soft landing areas), gymnastic mats, etc.

5 **Environmental factors** – these were covered earlier (topic 3), but would specifically apply in any challenge activities included in outdoor and adventurous activities.

6 **Rules** – all physical activities have rules and these include specific ones designed to make sure that injuries do not occur. **For example, the enforced wearing of shin pads in football minimises leg and shin injuries and the wearing of batting helmets in cricket minimises head injuries.** Other general rules set out how performers have to play correctly and fairly – foul play is likely to result in injuries occurring. The governing bodies for each activity set out the specific precautions and rules they expect to be in place for that activity and it is a primary responsibility of the officials in charge to make sure that these are considered and observed. **For example, in football, a referee's assistant will check the condition of players' studs before they are allowed to enter the field of play.**

7   **Code of conduct** – the ways in which activities are carried out and the expectations which are introduced and enforced are important; **for example, the ways in which javelins are thrown and then collected.**

8   **Appropriate warm-ups and cool-downs** – an essential precaution to avoid injury, especially the warm-up. It is a crucial factor in preparation and its main purpose is to reduce the possibility of injuries occurring.

Common injuries

Revised

No matter how many precautions are taken there is still the possibility of accidents occurring, such as the following:

- **Impact injuries** – these are caused when any form of contact occurs. This could be the strike of a cricket/rounders ball or impact with another player/performer, or even with the playing surface following a fall or dive.

- **Internally caused injuries** – this can include overuse injuries such as tennis elbow or stress fractures. It is also fairly common for performers to experience sudden injuries such as **strains** or **sprains** – pulled hamstrings often occur.

Key terms

Strain – the overstretching of a muscle

Sprain – the overstretching or tearing of ligaments at a joint

Exam tip

The examiner is likely to ask questions relating to how injuries might be prevented. Make sure you can give specific examples from specific activities with some explanation of the type of injury which might occur.

Check your understanding

Tested

1   Choose a physical activity and give an example where using a correct action could help to prevent an injury.   *(4 marks)*

2   Give an example from a physical activity where a player should wear specific protective clothing and describe how it can prevent injury.   *(4 marks)*

3   An example of an overuse injury is a:

    a   fracture

    b   bruise

    c   cut

    d   stress fracture.   *(1 mark)*

8. Aerobic and anaerobic exercise

The respiratory system is the body's system for air entering and leaving the body. Respiration is the process of gaseous exchange in which oxygen is taken in from the air (inspiration) and exchanged for carbon dioxide, before it is then breathed out (expiration).

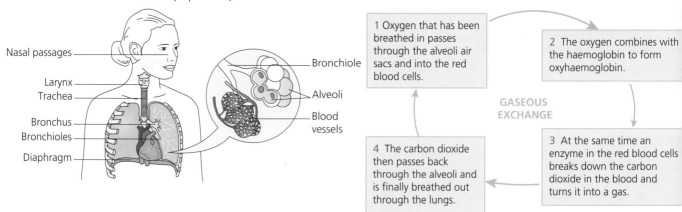

Nasal passages

Larynx
Trachea

Bronchus
Bronchioles

Diaphragm

Bronchiole

Alveoli

Blood vessels

1 Oxygen that has been breathed in passes through the alveoli air sacs and into the red blood cells.

2 The oxygen combines with the haemoglobin to form oxyhaemoglobin.

GASEOUS EXCHANGE

4 The carbon dioxide then passes back through the alveoli and is finally breathed out through the lungs.

3 At the same time an enzyme in the red blood cells breaks down the carbon dioxide in the blood and turns it into a gas.

↑ **The respiratory system and gaseous exchange**

Aerobic exercise   Revised ☐

Aerobic respiration is respiration in the presence of oxygen and is summarised as:

Glucose + oxygen → energy + carbon dioxide + water

This type of respiration is used when the body is exercising for a long period of time and the energy for this exercise is produced using oxygen. Aerobic exercise makes full use of the respiratory system to make sure that sufficient oxygen is being taken in throughout the exercise period.

Anaerobic exercise   Revised ☐

Anaerobic respiration is respiration in the absence of oxygen and is summarised as:

Glucose → energy + lactic acid

This type of respiration is used when the body works without sufficient oxygen being supplied to the muscles. As oxygen is not being used to generate the energy, anaerobic respiration can only be used for short periods of exercise.

Exam tip

Make sure you know the difference between aerobic and anaerobic exercise and can give an example of each. Learn the formula for each type of respiration.

Function of the blood

Revised

The blood transports oxygen, glucose and waste products round the body. It also assists with body temperature control and protection. In aerobic exercise the blood carries oxygen to the muscles, whereas in anaerobic exercise the blood cannot transport enough oxygen quickly enough to the muscles.

Oxygen debt

Revised

During anaerobic exercise the body runs out of sufficient supplies of oxygen and the glycogen stores are used as an alternative energy supply. Lactic acid (a mild poison) builds up in the working muscles. During recovery the oxygen debt must be repaid – additional oxygen, above what is usually required when at rest, must be consumed.

The recovery process

Revised

Straight after exercise the body has to be allowed to recover. Large amounts of breath are expired and this removes the carbon dioxide and other waste products from the lungs. Perspiration occurs as a form of temperature control: the evaporation of sweat reduces the heat of the body. An effective cool-down also allows the lactic acid to disperse safely.

Check your understanding

Tested

1 Anaerobic respiration will be used in a:

   a marathon run

   b 100-metre sprint

   c cross-country run

   d 100-metre swimming race. *(1 mark)*

2 Describe three different functions of the blood. *(3 marks)*

3 What is lactic acid and how can you effectively remove it from the body? *(4 marks)*

9. The circulatory system

The circulatory system is the movement of blood around the body. It is closely linked to the respiratory system. Together the two systems are called the **cardiovascular system**.

The heart
Revised

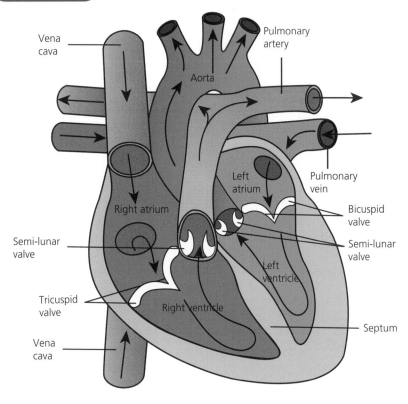

↑ The heart

The heart is basically a muscular pump which acts in the following way:

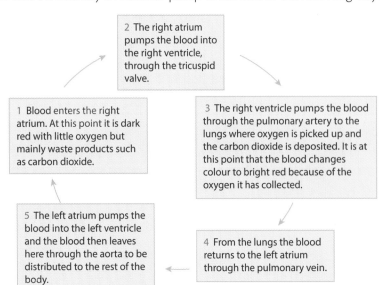

2 The right atrium pumps the blood into the right ventricle, through the tricuspid valve.

1 Blood enters the right atrium. At this point it is dark red with little oxygen but mainly waste products such as carbon dioxide.

3 The right ventricle pumps the blood through the pulmonary artery to the lungs where oxygen is picked up and the carbon dioxide is deposited. It is at this point that the blood changes colour to bright red because of the oxygen it has collected.

5 The left atrium pumps the blood into the left ventricle and the blood then leaves here through the aorta to be distributed to the rest of the body.

4 From the lungs the blood returns to the left atrium through the pulmonary vein.

- **Arteries** – these have thick walls and carry oxygenated blood at high pressure away from the heart. They have no valves and their walls are more elastic than the walls of veins. They sub-divide into smaller vessels known as arterioles.

- **Veins** – these carry deoxygenated blood back to the heart and their walls are thinner and less elastic than the walls of arteries. Veins have valves to make sure the blood is not able to flow backwards.

- **Capillaries** – these are microscopic vessels that allow carbon dioxide, oxygen and waste products to pass through their very thin walls.

Exam tip

The examiner will not ask specific questions about the heart and its chambers. However, knowing how the blood is transported throughout the body via the blood vessels will help you to answer questions relating to effective training methods and the effect of exercise on the body.

Check your understanding

1 Which of the following is not a blood vessel?

   a   Plasma

   b   Capillaries

   c   Veins

   d   Arteries   *(1 mark)*

2 Explain the differences between an artery and a vein.   *(4 marks)*

10. Leisure and recreation

Leisure and recreation combine as a key part of a balanced and healthy lifestyle.

Exam tip

You need to know the *characteristics* and *benefits* of leisure and to be able to identify the differences between the two terms.

Leisure
Revised

This is the free time that you have when not working or at school – time in which you are free to choose what you want to do. People generally have more leisure time now than they did in the past and there are now many more organisations that provide for both active leisure (low-level physical activities such as yoga or walking) and passive leisure; **for example, going to the cinema or theatre, or even just staying in and watching television**.

Labour-saving devices mean more leisure time.

Recreation
Revised

Recreation describes activities carried out during leisure time.

- **Physical recreation** – individuals take part in these activities for **intrinsic rewards** rather than **extrinsic** ones. The health benefits and enjoyment aspects are more important than competitive success or gain.

- **Outdoor recreation** – many of these types of activities are associated with some level of challenge and involve making use of the natural environment. They include walking, climbing and caving. Water-based activities are also popular in this category, such as sailing, windsurfing, swimming and canoeing.

Key terms

Intrinsic reward – something that gives an individual an internal satisfaction achieved from doing something well

Extrinsic reward – something done for a particular reward which is clearly visible to others and which can be seen as an achievement

One of the aims of encouraging individuals to make active use of their leisure time through participating in recreational activities is to promote the notion of lifetime sports. These are sports that can be enjoyed at any age.

Check your understanding _____ Tested ☐

1 All of the following are extrinsic rewards except for:

   a   an achievement certificate

   b   a personal feeling of achievement

   c   a medal

   d   a trophy.   *(1 mark)*

2 Which of the following would not be considered to be an active leisure activity?

   a   Going to the cinema

   b   Walking

   c   Attending a Pilates class

   d   Taking part in a yoga session   *(1 mark)*

3 What is the difference between leisure and recreation?   *(2 marks)*

11. Health and fitness

Health and fitness

The World Health Organization's definition of health is: 'a state of complete physical, mental and social wellbeing and not merely the absence of disease or infirmity'. Fitness is 'the capability of the body to meet the daily demands made upon it with some comfort/without stress' (from AQA teacher's notes, page 8).

Fitness is one aspect of general health. There are different types of fitness:

- **General fitness** – a level of fitness suitable for a club standard performer
- **Specific fitness** – the level of fitness required for an international standard performer in the same activity

Regular exercise maintains both health and fitness as part of a healthy, active lifestyle. A healthy, active lifestyle:

- helps to provide the levels of strength and stamina needed for everyday life; for example, jobs that involve repeated manual tasks such as stacking shelves, or jobs that require you to be on your feet all day
- maintains basic levels of flexibility to be able to cope with everyday living and without suffering discomfort; for example, being able to bend sufficiently to tie up shoelaces or reach up to get a book from a shelf
- should enable the individual to maintain a good level of fitness.

While people with jobs involving manual labour are already taking regular exercise as part of what they do, many people today have **sedentary** jobs. And while some people have outdoor jobs, most people work inside, away from fresh air and natural light. So, for a lot of people, a healthy, active lifestyle involves making choices, for example:

- walking or cycling to work or school, instead of using a car or public transport
- taking part in some active leisure pursuits, such as swimming or other sports.

> **Key term**
>
> **Sedentary** – sitting down or being physically inactive for long periods of time

↑ **Many outdoor jobs ensure a healthy, active lifestyle**

> **Exam tip**
>
> Make sure you can explain how a healthy, active lifestyle can contribute to an individual's health and fitness.

Exercise guidelines

Revised

How much exercise someone can do is connected to the physical condition they are in and also what they want to achieve from regular exercise over time.

Effects of exercise

Revised

Exercise has the following short-term effects on the body:

● The breathing rate and the **heart rate** increase.

● The body temperature increases – sweating occurs.

● There can be slight reddening of the skin.

● Some tiredness or a feeling of heaviness is felt in some of the muscles.

You can use your knowledge of body systems like the muscular and skeletal systems to help explain the effects exercise has on the body.

> **Key term**
>
> **Heart rate** – the number of times the heart beats in one minute. For the average resting adult the heart rate is approximately 72 beats per minute.

> **Exam tip**
>
> The examiner is likely to ask questions regarding the differences between health and fitness and the ways in which they are related.

Check your understanding

Tested

1 Which of the following would *not* be considered to be a sedentary job?

   a   Office worker

   b   Lorry driver

   c   Telesales worker

   d   Farmer   (1 mark)

2 Which of the following would *not* be an active, healthy lifestyle choice?

   a   Cycling to school or work

   b   Getting on and of bus stops at earlier or later stops in order to walk part of the journey

   c   Always using escalators instead of stairs

   d   Volunteering for some manual labour jobs   (1 mark)

3 Define what is meant by good health.   (3 marks)

4 Why is it important to have flexibility for everyday living?   (3 marks)

12. The skeletal system

Health, fitness and the skeletal system

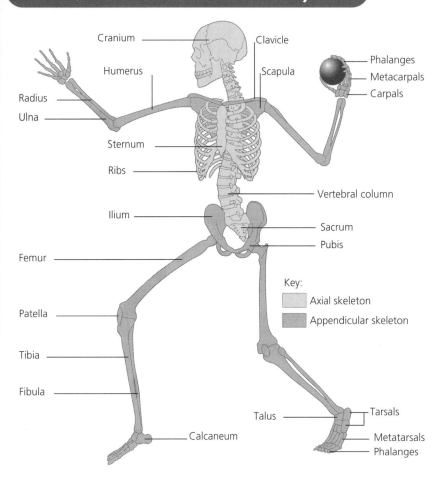

Cranium
Clavicle
Humerus
Scapula
Radius
Ulna
Sternum
Ribs
Ilium
Femur
Patella
Tibia
Fibula
Talus
Calcaneum
Phalanges
Metacarpals
Carpals
Vertebral column
Sacrum
Pubis
Tarsals
Metatarsals
Phalanges

Key:
- Axial skeleton
- Appendicular skeleton

↑ The skeletal system

The main bones of the skeletal system are shown on the diagram above. The skeletal system has three functions in relation to physical activity:

1 Support

2 Movement

3 Protection

The skeletal system provides a framework within which movement can occur and this movement clearly contributes to any performance.

Movement can only occur at the **joints**. Different types of movement occur in the different types of joint:

- **Ball and socket** – these are the joints at the shoulder (scapula, clavicle and humerus) and the hips (femur and ilium). The movements of **abduction** and **adduction** can take place here.

- **Hinge** – these are the joints at the knee (femur, patella and tibia) and the elbow (humerus, radius and ulna). The movements of **flexion** and **extension** occur here.

Protection occurs where vital organs are protected, such as the cranium protecting the brain and the ribs protecting the heart and lungs.

Key terms

Joint – a connection point between two bones where movement occurs

Abduction – the movement of a bone or limb away from the body

Adduction – the movement of a bone or limb towards the body

Flexion – when the angle between two bones is decreased

Extension – when the angle between two bones is increased

These joints are known as freely moveable joints and they are the ones which allow the movements in sports actions to occur.

The rib cage moves during the action of breathing and respiration (see topic 8) as air is inspired and expired.

(see topic 8)

Check your understanding

Tested

1 All of the following are functions of the skeleton except:

   a size

   b support

   c movement

   d protection.   *(1 mark)*

2 Bending your arm at the elbow is known as what?

   a Adduction

   b Flexion

   c Extension

   d Abduction   *(1 mark)*

3 Which one of the following is an example of a hinge joint?

   a Shoulder

   b Hip

   c Knee

   d Wrist   *(1 mark)*

4 Which three joints would be primarily involved in throwing a ball?   *(3 marks)*

13. The muscular system

Health, fitness and the muscular system

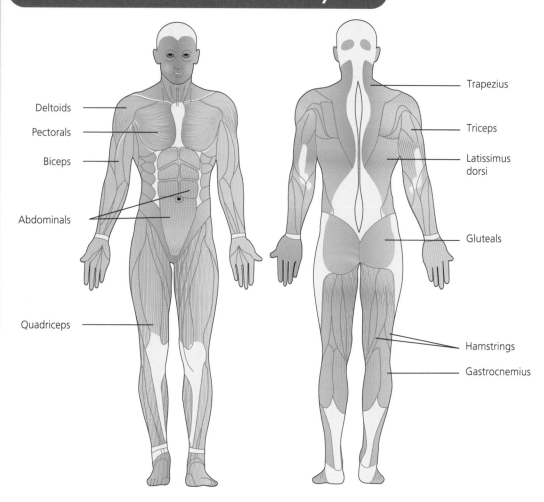

Deltoids
Pectorals
Biceps
Abdominals
Quadriceps

Trapezius
Triceps
Latissimus dorsi
Gluteals
Hamstrings
Gastrocnemius

↑ **The main muscles**

The muscular system and skeletal system combine to allow movement to occur. To do this they make use of connective tissues known as **ligaments** and **tendons**.

Muscles have to be arranged in pairs as they cannot push – they only pull.

● The prime mover (or **agonist**) is the muscle which initially contracts to start a movement.

● The **antagonist** is the muscle which relaxes to allow a movement to take place.

One example is the bending movement at the elbow. The antagonist is the triceps, which relaxes and slightly lengthens, while the biceps is the prime mover, as it contracts and appears to get smaller as it bulges. You can feel these movements in your own arm if you grip loosely around the muscles. See diagram on opposite page.

Key terms

Ligaments – bands of fibres that are attached to the bones and link the joints together

Tendons – very strong cords that join the muscle to the bone

Agonist – the muscle that contracts to allow a movement to take place

Antagonist – the muscle that relaxes to allow a movement to take place

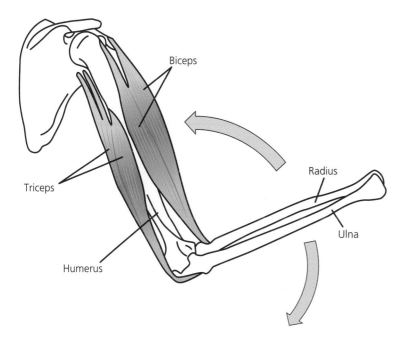

↑ The muscles involved in bending the elbow

You only need to know about certain muscles and the main movements which occur at them:

- **Biceps and triceps** – any arm movements, such as throwing
- **Hamstrings and quadriceps** – movements of the legs, such as running and kicking
- **Deltoids** – allow shoulder movement, used a lot in swimming
- **Trapezius** – helps to keep the shoulder in position, used in a soccer throw-in
- **Latissimus dorsi** – allow shoulder movement backwards, forwards, up and down
- **Pectorals** – at the front of the upper chest, so often used in throwing actions such as the javelin
- **Abdominals** – used to allow bending and turning of the trunk section; very important 'stabilising' muscles relating to 'core strength'

Exam tip

It is useful to know about certain muscles and the main movements that occur at them. However, exam questions will focus on how the muscular system is involved in movement and how the muscular and skeletal systems combine together to allow movement.

Check your understanding   Tested

1 Which of the following best describes the role of tendons?
   a They attach muscles to bones.
   b They attach muscles to muscles.
   c They attach bones to bones.
   d They attach ligaments to bones.   (1 mark)

2 The muscle which relaxes to allow a movement to take place is the:
   a prime mover
   b agonist
   d flexor
   e antagonist.   (1 mark)

3 Identify two major muscle groups of the upper body used when performing a standing throw of a ball.   (2 marks)

4 Explain how an active lifestyle can keep muscles healthy.   (4 marks)

14. Fitness components

Fitness is made up of different components – strength, speed, stamina, etc. These components are used differently at different times to meet different demands, usually in various combinations.

Strength ——————————————————————————— Revised ☐

Every individual needs a degree of **strength** to deal with the efforts and loads placed upon and experienced by the body. There are three main types of strength:

1 **Dynamic strength** – this is the strength an individual needs to sustain their own body weight over a prolonged period of time, or to be able to apply some force against an object; **for example, a gymnast performing a pommel horse routine.**

2 **Explosive strength** – this is muscular strength used in one short, sharp movement; **for example, a long jumper leaving the take-off board.**

3 **Static strength** – this is the greatest amount of strength that can be applied to an immovable object; **for example, the forwards pushing against each other in a rugby scrum.**

Most activities require a combination of up to all three of these types of strength.

Key term

Strength – the maximum force that can be developed within a muscle or group of muscles during a single maximal contraction

Speed ——————————————————————————— Revised ☐

Speed is the ability to move all or parts of the body as quickly as possible. Speed is also linked to reaction time, another component of fitness. In order to have speed, a performer needs to be able to contract their muscles quickly to be able to perform movements as swiftly as possible.

Power ——————————————————————————— Revised ☐

This is the combination of the maximum amount of speed with the maximum amount of strength. Remember that power can only be used in short bursts and not maintained over long periods of time.

Stamina ——————————————————————————— Revised ☐

Stamina is required by performers who are taking part in physical activities that require them to maintain effort over a period of time. Stamina is often known as 'endurance'.

There are two types of endurance:

1 **Cardiovascular endurance** – this is the ability of the heart and lungs to keep supplying oxygen in the bloodstream to provide the energy to carry on with physical movement. **For example, a cross-country runner needs high levels of cardiovascular endurance.**

2 **Muscular endurance** – this is the ability of a muscle, or a group of muscles, to keep working against a resistance. **For example, a climber on a steep climb requires high levels of muscular endurance.**

Flexibility
Revised

Flexibility is the range of movement at and around a joint. Performers need high levels of flexibility and **suppleness** to be able to move their joints through their full range. Levels of flexibility do differ between individuals and the full range of movement at joints is not something which everyone is able to achieve.

> **Key term**
>
> **Suppleness** – when your muscles and joints work together so well that you can achieve the maximum range of movement without any pain or injury

Balance
Revised

Balance is the ability to retain the centre of mass of the body above the base of support. It is also the ability to maintain a particular shape or posture while staying level and stable. Balance is very important for a performer in maintaining control, shape and alignment.

Co-ordination
Revised

Co-ordination is the ability to link all the parts of a movement into one efficient smooth movement; it is the ability to control the body during physical activity. Good co-ordination means that two or more body parts are being used together. This is essential for a performer to be able to maintain their balance and also achieve an effective interaction of movements.

Agility
Revised

Agility is the combination of flexibility and speed and means a performer can swiftly change the position of their body, including changes in direction and speed. It allows the performer to move quickly and **nimbly**.

> **Key term**
>
> **Nimble** – quick and light in movement; able to move with ease and rapidly

← This gymnast is effectively combining flexibility, balance and agility in this movement

Reaction time

The reaction time is how quickly a performer can respond to something. It is the time taken for the body, or parts of the body, to respond to a stimulus.

↑ This sprinter has made good use of reaction time when the starting pistol went off, and explosive strength to move off from the starting blocks

Timing

Timing is the ability to produce the correct movement at the optimum time and to coincide movements in relation to external factors. This component also makes use of reaction time and co-ordination. **For example, a cricketer timing their swing for optimum contact with the ball is a good example of effective timing.**

1 All of the following are types of strength apart from:

   a   static

   b   enduring

   c   dynamic

   d   explosive.   *(1 mark)*

2 Flexibility is best described as:

   a   having bendy bones

   b   moving at a joint

   c   the range of movement an individual has

   d   the range of movement at a joint.   *(1 mark)*

3 All of the following would be an advantage to a sprinter apart from:

   a   endurance

   b   reaction time

   c   explosive strength

   d   speed.   *(1 mark)*

4 What is meant by good timing and how would this be of particular advantage to a tennis player?   *(4 marks)*

15. Training types and programmes

Individuals regularly train and take part in training programmes because they are aware of the effects this training and exercise has on their bodies and the ways in which it can improve their levels of performance.

Training programmes

Each training programme listed and described has its own particular advantages and disadvantages. Individuals undertake training programmes in order to improve their fitness, skills and techniques.

Weight training

Taking part in weight training has the advantage of:

- improving **muscle tone**
- increasing muscular endurance
- developing muscle size, or bulk
- assisting recovery after injury.

When taking part in weight training it is important to be aware of the following terms:

- **Repetitions** – this is the number of times you move the weights when training. If using barbells then one barbell curl would equal one repetition.
- **Set** – this is the number of repetitions you carry out for a particular weight activity without stopping. So, each time you complete your repetitions of the barbell curls, you have completed one set.

The ways in which the combination of repetitions and sets is used will affect the outcome of the training. The general rule is that for exercise to improve muscle tone you should use fairly light weights but have a fairly high number of repetitions for about three sets. For more specific strength improvement, which would include building up muscle bulk, you would choose heavier weights with a small number of repetitions and an increased number of sets.

The disadvantages of weight training are as follows:

- Equipment can often be very specialised, expensive and bulky – it takes up a lot of space.
- To be performed correctly, especially with 'free weights', a training partner is needed to assist.

> **Key term**
>
> **Muscle tone** – the tension which remains in a muscle, even when at rest

This is one of the most popular and common forms of training, mainly because it is very flexible and versatile.

The main advantages of circuit training are that:

● equipment can be very basic, simply benches and mats; it is even possible to run some circuits without any equipment at all

● various components of fitness can be worked on and targeted for improvement, such as strength, power, flexibility, endurance and agility

● a wide range of exercises and activities can be included – this reduces the boredom factor!

● the training principle of overload can be used easily (see topic 16)

● the circuit can be tailored to each individual's need, taking into account various fitness levels and work levels

● both aerobic and anaerobic activities can be included

● all group sizes can be catered for, ranging from an individual to a large group of 40 or more.

↑ A circuit training class showing a variety of exercises

Running a circuit

● The areas (called stations) need to be clearly laid out and labelled to show which exercise or activity is to be performed at each station.

● The activities/movements should be correctly demonstrated so that correct techniques are used.

● The activities performed must be varied so that similar exercises do not follow each other – this is to allow muscle groups some time to recover.

● Each circuit 'lap' must have rest periods included so that 'work times' and 'rest times' allow the performers a brief period of recovery before moving on to the next station.

● Circuits can be set up to target skills or fitness, or a combination of the two.

● Circuits can be timed (each activity and rest period has a set time allocated to it) or fixed load (the number of exercises/activities is set).

The main disadvantages of circuit training are that it is very difficult to carry out on your own and it often takes quite a long time to set up and run.

Interval training

Revised

This is a form of training that consists of periods of work followed by periods of rest – it commonly involves running. Its main advantage is that it does not require any specialist equipment, it allows individuals to train on their own and it is well suited to anaerobic-type activities.

The combinations for interval training include:

● work/time duration – this could be the distance of the run, or the length of time of a run

● the intensity of the work – this could be the speed at which the run occurs

● repetitions – this could be the number of work repetitions or even the rest ones

● recovery time duration – this usually refers to a period of time but it can also be distance, such as a measured slow walk.

The main disadvantage of interval training is that it is very specific and not related to general fitness.

Continuous training

Revised

This is designed primarily to improve endurance as it keeps the heart and **pulse rate** high throughout an extended period. The intention is to make sure that the body's demand for oxygen is matched by its oxygen uptake, which then targets aerobic fitness.

The main advantages of this training are ease of setting up and very specific outcomes for individuals. The main disadvantage is that is a very specific type of training and therefore not suitable for general training.

Key term

Pulse rate – the rate per minute at which the heart beats which can be located and measured at certain points in the body

Fartlek training

Revised

Fartlek is a Swedish word which means 'speed training' and refers to a form of continuous training. It alternates walking, brisk walking, running, jogging and fast, steady running. It originated in the Scandinavian countryside where it often involved running up hills.

It shares the same advantages and disadvantages as continuous training.

Exam tip

The examiner is likely to ask questions about which particular training method would be most suitable for a particular type of sport or physical activity. You will need to give reasons as to why it would be the most suitable method.

General considerations

Revised

There are some factors which need to be taken into account whichever form of training is undertaken.

Training thresholds

This is the point at which the training being undertaken actually starts to improve levels of physical fitness.

The maximum heart rate (MHR) is the highest level you can attain. It is calculated using the formula of 220 minus the individual's age. So, for a sixteen-year-old, the calculation would be 220 − 16 = 204.

Heart rate training zones

The diagram below shows the training zones which can be used. In order to improve levels of cardiovascular endurance (and therefore aerobic capacity) you need to train at a fairly high level and keep the heart rate up at that level for at least fifteen minutes.

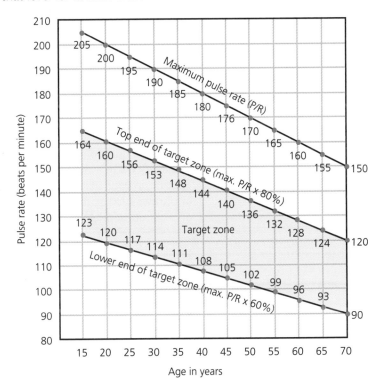

↑ **Training zones**

Environment

The training environment covers, for example, the altitude or the temperature at which the training takes place. Many performers choose to carry out 'warm weather' training, which allows them to train in more comfortable conditions. It can also take into account the training year for a performer in terms of whether their activity has a closed season, set dates for competitions or requirements for pre-season preparation.

Check your understanding   Tested

1 Using the correct calculation, work out what the maximum heart rate would be for a fifteen-year-old. *(3 marks)*

2 All of the following are advantages of taking a weight training programme except for:

   a improvement of muscle tone

   b improvement of agility

   c improvement of muscular endurance

   d increase of muscle size. *(1 mark)*

3 Using examples, explain the difference between repetitions and sets. *(4 marks)*

4 Explain why similar exercises should not be placed next to each other in a circuit training programme. *(3 marks)*

16. Principles of training

Specificity

Specificity within a training programme will vary according to the type of:

- person who is training – it will depend on their initial fitness levels, body type and physiological factors, as well as other individual differences
- activity being trained for – it will depend on the sport itself and the level at which it is to be performed.

Key term

Specificity – the particular kind of activity or exercise you use to build up or improve certain body systems or skills

Exam tip

If you get a question about specificity try to avoid the word 'specific' in your answer. Use words or phrases such as 'most suited to' or 'most appropriate'.

Progression

You must build **progression** into a training programme and always bear in mind the following points:

- The levels of general and specific fitness in place at the start of the programme must be taken into account.
- You may have to start very gradually but you must increase the demands as your body adjusts to the work it is doing and the stresses it is experiencing.
- **Plateauing** occurs when you progress to a certain level then seem to get stuck there before being able to move on – this can happen more than once.

Key term

Progression – gradually and safely increasing the amount of training that you do

Plateauing – progressing to a certain level then seeming to get stuck there before being able to move on

Overload

Overload is usually linked to the FIT acronym, which stands for:

- **F** – frequency, or how often training takes place; training more often increases overload
- **I** – intensity, of how hard you train; extra amounts of activity or increasing weights (if these are being used) increases overload
- **T** – the time, or duration, of each session; increasing the actual amount of time spent training, or even on one particular aspect of the training, also increases overload.

An important factor linked to overload is that of safety. **Progressive overload** ensures that the additional demands are added only gradually and safely.

Key term

Overload – making your body work harder than normal in order to make it adapt or improve

Progressive overload – where additional demands are added only gradually and safely

Exam tip

Remember that overload is a positive aspect and one which is to be encouraged when training. It is not to be confused with 'overuse', which can cause injuries.

Reversibility

Reversibility will be felt if, for any reason, training either stops or is reduced.

- Positive effects will be lost at roughly the rate of one-third of the time it took to gain them!

- A beginner loses effects at a faster rate than a regular, trained performer.

- Different factors of fitness may be affected in different ways and to different degrees.

Key term

Reversibility – the loss of positive effects if you stop training

Sometimes reversibility may be forced through injury!

Check your understanding

1 Which one of the following is the best description of the specificity training principle while weight training?

   a   Increasing the weights lifted for each training session

   b   Concentrating on training muscles of the upper arm

   c   Lifting your maximum weight for one repetition

   d   Using all free weights rather than machines   *(1 mark)*

2 Which one of the following best describes the frequency element of the FIT principle of training?

   a   How hard you exercise

   b   The type of exercise you choose

   c   How much time you take to exercise

   d   How many times a week you exercise   *(1 mark)*

3 The main training principles are: specificity, overload, progression and reversibility. Describe *two* of these training principles and give a practical example for each.   *(6 marks)*

17. Diet

It is essential to maintain a balanced diet so that the body is able to receive the nourishment it needs to be able to maintain good physical health.

Maintaining a balanced diet

Everyone needs food to survive and nutrients are the substances that make up food. The correct mixture of food and nutrients needs to be consumed.

The eatwell plate

Use the eatwell plate to help you get the balance right. It shows how much of what you eat should come from each food group.

FOOD STANDARDS AGENCY
food.gov.uk

Fruit and vegetables

Bread, rice, potatoes, pasta and other starchy foods

Meat, fish, eggs, beans and other non-dairy sources of protein

Foods and drinks high in fat and/or sugar

Milk and dairy foods

↑ **This represents the nutrients that make up a balanced diet and also includes the appropriate portion sizes**

Carbohydrates

These are the main energy source for the body and there are two categories of these:

1. Simple carbohydrates found in foods such as sugar, milk and fruit
2. Complex carbohydrates found in foods such as bread, pasta, potatoes, rice and pulses/beans

Carbohydrates are stored as glycogen in the liver and muscles. Glycogen can be used to provide energy during exercise.

Endurance athletes and performers often **carbo-load** (also known as carbohydrate-loading) as a way of preparing themselves for a particular event or competition in order to increase their energy levels.

Key term

Carbo-load – eating foods that are high in starch to increase carbohydrate reserves in muscles

Proteins

These are often called 'building blocks' because they are so important in the growth of new tissue. They are very important for muscle growth and repair.

Proteins are obtained from two sources:

1. Animal protein from fish, chicken and red meat
2. Vegetable protein from pulses (beans), grains and foods produced from animal products such as eggs, milk and cheese

Some performers will select a **high protein diet**. These are usually bodybuilders or weightlifters aiming to build muscle and lose fat.

Key term

High protein diet – a diet made up of a lot of protein and a reduced intake of carbohydrates and fats. Has been linked to kidney problems.

Vitamins

Vitamins are essential to enable you to maintain good health. Only small quantities are needed and these are usually contained in a normal healthy diet.

There are a great many different vitamins (all given a letter of the alphabet as they were discovered) but you only need to know about the following:

● **Vitamin A** – this is a fat-soluble vitamin found in milk and dairy products and it can be stored in the body. It helps to maintain healthy eyes, skin and bones.

● **Vitamin C** – this is a water-soluble vitamin so it cannot be stored in the body. A lack of vitamin C can cause scurvy.

● **Vitamin D** – this is another fat-soluble vitamin so it can be stored in the body and it can also be produced naturally (from sunlight). A deficiency of vitamin D can cause rickets.

Minerals

These are essential for health and bone and connective tissue formation. You only need to know about three types:

1 **Iodine** – this is needed for hormone formation, notably from the thyroid gland.

2 **Iron** – this is needed for the transport of oxygen by the red blood cells.

3 **Calcium** – this is contained in dark green leafy vegetables, broccoli, milk products and salmon and is essential for strong bones, muscle contraction and relaxation, blood clotting and nerve function.

Exam tip

The examiner will only ask questions relating to vitamins A, C and D, and iodine, iron and calcium as minerals. This also means that this is all you will need to refer to in any diet questions asked.

Fats

Fats are a source of energy and also help to insulate the body and to keep the body temperature at the right level. There are three types of fats:

1 Saturates

2 Mono-unsaturates

3 Polyunsaturates

Fats are found in many foods, including cheese, cream, meat and cooking oils, butter and margarine.

It is important to control the amount of fat in the diet because too much fat can be the main cause of gaining overall body weight.

Water/fluids

The human body is mostly water (about 70 per cent) and on average we lose about 2.5 litres of water from our body every day.

Water is a means of transport for nutrients, waste and hormones. Failure to replace water can result in dehydration, which can cause serious problems such as heat exhaustion. It is important to replace the water you lose by drinking. If you fail to do so your body will weaken to the point where it will stop functioning.

The following will affect how quickly water is lost:

● The intensity of any work or exercise being carried out

● The amount of time spent exercising

● The temperature and humidity of your environment

Fibre/roughage

Fibre is important as it aids the digestive system and also adds some bulk to food. It is contained in wholegrain cereals, wholegrain bread, oats, fruits and vegetables.

Energy equations

The amount of energy you use is a factor to consider in terms of diet. You also need some energy just to keep your body working at rest.

Your basal metabolic rate is the amount of energy needed for important processes such as breathing and keeping the heart beating. If you do not balance the intake and output of energy you can suffer from one of the following:

- **Obesity** – being extremely overweight
- **Anorexia** – being extremely underweight
- **Malnutrition** – extreme weight loss

Specific requirements for different performers
Revised

Dietary needs vary between people taking part in different physical activities, and performers need to be aware of this and vary their diet accordingly. Some examples are as follows:

- Female gymnasts need to be small and light and therefore should be careful to avoid too much fatty food.
- A weightlifter needs to be quite large and bulky so additional fats and proteins may be needed.
- A soccer player has to make sure that they have enough energy-providing food for a 90-minute game.
- A marathon runner may have a high carbohydrate diet and specifically carbo-load for several days just before a race. They may even attend specially organised pasta parties to help them prepare.

When you eat is also an important factor and the following should be taken into account:

- Before activity – it is not wise to eat too close to taking part in physical activity and a performer should wait for two hours after eating.
- During activity – generally it is not recommended to eat during physical activity, although small quantities, for example fruit such as bananas, are all right.
- After activity – the same two-hour gap should be left after physical activity before eating substantial amounts. However, drinking liquids straight away is a good thing.

Planning a diet for a sports performer is usually a long-term exercise and is often carried out over a substantial period of time.

Check your understanding
Tested

1 Which of the following is *not* a basic component of a healthy balanced diet?

   a Carbohydrates   c Fats

   b Calories   d Proteins   *(1 mark)*

2 Explain what is meant by 'basal metabolic rate'.   *(3 marks)*

3 For the following two specific diets, identify the type of sport each would be most appropriate for:

   a Plenty of carbohydrates, including attending a pasta party and carbo-loading just before an event

   b Avoiding too many fatty foods in order to keep body weight regulated, but ensuring that enough proteins and carbohydrates are included to maintain energy levels

                                                       (2 marks)

4 Why do the organisers of marathon races place water stations at regular intervals along the route? *(2 marks)*

18. School influences

This topic is about the factors that influence people to get involved in healthy physical activities – for example, cultural factors (see topic 2). Schools can be a very important influence.

National Curriculum requirements

Revised

It is a legal requirement for PE to be taught at school. Most schools also provide exam courses, like GCSE PE, for their students. The reasons for this are:

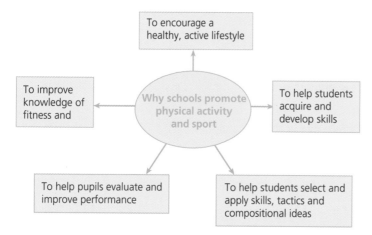

All schools provide a range of physical activities designed to develop the strength, stamina, suppleness (flexibility) and speed of the upper body and arms and the lower body and legs. Schools are required to achieve these aims through at least two hours a week of focused activities. This is usually known by the term 'core curriculum', which is delivered through timetabled lessons, but some schools will provide more than this minimum requirement.

> **Exam tip**
>
> The examiner is likely to ask questions specifically regarding why schools offer PE and the benefits it can bring.

The healthy schools programme and PSHE

Revised

The healthy schools programme is based on a whole-school approach to physical and emotional wellbeing. It is linked to the following four themes.

PSHE

PSHE stands for personal, social and health education and includes the following:

● Sex and relationship education as well as drug education

● Linking to the general National Curriculum outcomes for pupils being healthy, staying safe, enjoying and achieving and making a positive contribution, and achieving economic wellbeing

● Providing knowledge, understanding, skills and attitudes to make informed decisions in life

Healthy eating

This includes the following:

- Being aware of what a balanced diet is in order to assist with good health and an understanding of the particular values and properties of the various nutrients which make up a balanced diet (see topic 17)
- Knowing the different food types and the nutrients they contain
- Any problems which can be caused by either an imbalance or deficiency in diet
- The whole school food policy, which includes the standards and requirements for school lunch and the food choices which schools make available

Physical activity

Each school has a physical activity policy which includes the following:

- A structure in place for two hours of physical activity
- Establishing a range of **extra-curricular activities:**
  - The activities a school provides will depend in part on the activities staff members are able to put on and are interested in providing.
  - The range and quality of facilities can be a factor.
  - Outside visits to other sporting providers, such as ice rinks and ten pin bowling centres, are encouraged.
  - Links to local clubs and activity providers, such as health clubs, golf clubs, etc., are encouraged.
  - A good range of leisure and recreation activities offered through teams, clubs and societies is also encouraged.

Emotional health and wellbeing

This includes supporting vulnerable individuals and groups, establishing a clear bullying policy, establishing behaviour and rewards policies and setting up pastoral support systems. Sport and physical activity are often very useful ways to improve people's emotional health as well as their physical health.

This is often all included in a school's safeguarding policy.

> **Key term**
>
> **Extra-curricular activity** – an activity that takes place out of timetabled lessons, such as pre-school, at lunchtime or after school

↑ After-school clubs provide opportunities to take part in physical activity

---

Check your understanding — Tested

1 Schools provide PE for all of the following reasons except:

   a to encourage extra-curricular participation

   b to provide sports performance awards

   c to encourage links with outside clubs

   d just to identify elite performers. *(1 mark)*

2 State two particular benefits of providing PE in timetabled school lessons. *(2 marks)*

3 What is meant by extra-curricular provision? Give an example. *(3 marks)*

19. Social and cultural factors

Social and cultural factors are very influential in affecting levels of participation in physical activity. They also shape an individual's attitude and approach to taking part.

Leisure time

The following factors are creating more opportunities for increased leisure time:

● Higher levels of unemployment

● Increasing levels of part-time work

● A shorter working week

● Technological advances, including labour-saving devices. This can also include advances in ICT and communication networks, which enable more people to work from home; this reduces travel time to and from work and therefore makes more time available.

All of this has, in turn, led to growth in the leisure industry in both the public and private sector in order to provide for this greater need.

● **Public sector** – these are facilities available to all individuals and are usually provided by local authorities such as local councils. There may be fees to take part but these are often quite low as they are subsidised (even free for some users); the public sector has only to break even with expenditure and not necessarily seek to make profits.

● **Private sector** – these are facilities that are privately owned, often by clubs or individuals. They usually charge membership fees and possibly additional fees as well, as they are businesses that are seeking to make a profit.

Both providers and users vary. Providers such as local authorities (therefore the public sector) will target particular 'user groups' such as:

● parents and toddlers

● unemployed workers

● shift workers

● other categories such as male or female only or particular age groups.

← **Parents and toddlers are a typical 'user group'**

These 'user groups' are targeted to ensure that the facilities provided are fully used. Concessions and allowances are often made for them, such as reduced fees or even free provision. Many local authorities also link with local health-care providers and even weight-loss organisations to emphasise the health-related benefits of taking part and to assist with recoveries from illnesses and medical conditions.

Exam tip

The examiner is likely to ask questions relating to why there is now more available leisure time and linking the provision made to specific identified 'user groups'.

Fairness and personal and social responsibility

Revised

In any sporting event there are concepts of **etiquette** and fairness which are expected from participants.

Some examples are as follows:

Key term

Etiquette – the unwritten rules or conventions of any activity

● General rules such as shaking hands with opponents, often at the start and the end of a match or competition

● Shaking hands with the officials, including umpires, referees and other minor officials

● Managers also joining in with handshakes with opponents and officials

● Footballers kicking the ball out of play when a player is injured. This enables play to be stopped for the injury to be treated and, following this, the opposition would be fair in return by returning the ball to the opponents who had stopped the play.

● Expectations in cricket for a batter to 'walk' when they know that they hit the ball for a catch

● Racket sports players calling double hits and 'not up' shots during a rally

A very important aspect of fairness and personal and social responsibility is for there to be high levels of mutual respect between players and officials. All participants are expected to adhere to the rules and spirit of the game and to respond positively to the officials who are in charge. This also includes maintaining this positive attitude with any teachers and coaches who are present.

Exam tip

Make sure you can explain what etiquette is and give an example of it from a sport or physical activity.

Social groupings

Revised

The main point to remember when considering the various social groupings is that they can all have both positive and negative effects on both attitudes and levels of participation.

Peers

The groups you mix with can be very influential regarding behaviour and actions. Peer pressure is often associated with teenagers in particular. **Peers** tend to have the following effects:

Key term

Peers – people who are the same age and status as you

● **Positive** – if your peers are very positive about participating in sport and physical activities it is likely that you will be influenced to take part too and that you will all, as a group, appreciate the benefits that can be gained.

● **Negative** – just as peers can encourage you to take part, the reverse can also be true. It can be difficult to ignore pressure from people trying to discourage you from taking part in sport and promoting other activities or attitudes instead.

Family

Family, especially parents, can have a big influence. Even before children go to school they may become interested in a sport or activity through their parents and family. Children often take up the sport their parents excelled in – many at national and international level!

Generally, family influence has a positive effect on participation:

- **Family members can assist with transport** – for many young people, being able to get to their sport or club can be one of the most difficult aspects relating to participation.
- **They can provide financial assistance** – this can be paying membership fees, buying sports clothing or providing specialist equipment.
- **They can provide support** – many parents go along to support their children when they are taking part and this encouragement can help to motivate a performance.

These positive factors are not always present. Family members may have a negative view of sport and participation – they may have had bad experiences themselves which has influenced their views. They may not be in a financial position to provide transport, clothing and equipment even if they would like to.

Gender

Social attitudes towards women used to have a negative influence on participation because it was considered wrong or dangerous for women to take part in some sports. However, in recent years attitudes towards women in sport have developed.

There is now a clear trend for there to be less sexual discrimination in sport. Laws are in place to make sure this does not happen and there are far fewer sports played only by men – **for example, the sports of cricket, rugby and football have seen a huge rise in interest, participation and organised sport and competition for women in recent years**. Social attitudes have also started to change in relation to women's participation in sports management and women taking official roles.

← Sian Massey is an English football referee who officiates as an assistant referee in the Premier League – the first female to officiate at this level. Her first Premiership game was in 2010

Ethnicity

In relation to physical activities, the **ethnic** origins of an individual can help to shape their awareness and appreciation of their own and others' cultures. This awareness and appreciation may be very positive but there are some cultures which can discourage participation in sport – often with particular reference to women (see topic 2).

> **Key term**
>
> **Ethnic** – relating to a group of people with a common national or cultural tradition

Check your understanding
Tested ☐

1 Which one of the following is *not* a reason for increased leisure time?

   a Labour-saving devices

   b Shorter working week

   c Peer pressure

   d Higher levels of unemployment   *(1 mark)*

2 Give *one* example of how local authorities target a particular 'user group' for leisure activities.   *(2 marks)*

3 What is meant by the term 'etiquette'? Give an example of a sportsperson displaying good etiquette.   *(3 marks)*

4 Describe *one* positive effect and *one* negative effect which family can have on participation levels for a school-age student.   *(4 marks)*

20. Opportunities and pathways

There are a number of ways in which it is possible for an individual to get involved, and stay involved, in physical activity.

Roles

Within the GCSE PE course there are opportunities to be assessed in various roles.

Player/performer

This is the main role available to an individual who wants to be fully and actively involved in physical activity as it involves physically participating. A player takes part in an activity which has levels of competition, teams and opponents, whereas a performer takes part in an activity such as dance or gymnastics.

Acquiring and utilising skills is important in this role and the individual must have a good knowledge of the tactics, playing positions, techniques and moves which are essential for their chosen activity. They would also need to be able to play/perform at different levels and cope with increasingly complex and demanding tasks. An individual has to develop the ability to make effective plans to improve their performance.

Leader/coach

This is a specialist in an activity who is responsible for preparing a performer/player in skill acquisition, correct technique and the correct physical or mental state. The individual undertaking this role has an important influence on individuals and/or groups in terms of their behaviour in sport and in helping them progress towards set goals.

Organiser

This role involves bringing together all the main ingredients at the right time, in the right place, in order to maximise promotion, participation and high quality performance.

Organisers need to be aware of all of the qualities expected from the players/performers but do not necessarily have to possess all of those qualities themselves.

Official

This is someone who controls the activity; they interpret the rules, laws or regulations of the activity, and are particularly responsible for checking the equipment.

Examples of officials include referees, umpires, judges, marshals, stewards, scorers, timekeepers and recorders. Most physical activities have different levels of officials, ranging from the senior ones (who are either mainly or solely in charge of an activity) to those known as 'minor officials', whose main responsibility is as assistants.

↑ An umpire in tennis is a good example of the role of official

> **Exam tip**
>
> You should know about the different roles that schools might encourage students to take on, and also what career possibilities might be available through specialising in PE.

Pathways

There are a number of pathways available for getting involved in physical activity. The National Curriculum lists the following:

These pathways can also include:

- accredited courses and qualifications (such as lifesaving, first aid and Sports Leaders Awards)
- examination-based courses (such as GCSE, BTEC), accreditation, sports performance awards, proficiency testing and awards
- cross-curricular possibilities, such as ICT
- cross-curricular work, such as health awareness and social education issues.

You may be particularly qualified or suited to take advantage of vocational opportunities; for example, the following regular occupations:

- Sports performer – either as a professional or an amateur. Some performers are able to take part in what is known as 'open sport', which enables both amateurs and professionals to compete together. When this happens the amateurs are not allowed to receive any prize money but they are able to claim expenses or even receive goods and prizes instead of money. These are considered to be some of the 'loopholes' which amateurs are able to take advantage of.
- Careers such as PE teacher, coach, trainer, physiotherapist, sports management

Key term

Accreditation – a formal official requirement which certifies your levels and qualifications

Check your understanding

Tested

1 All of the following are available roles within a GCSE PE course except:

  a player

  b manager

  c official

  d organiser.

(1 mark)

2 All of the following are types of officials except:

  a umpires

  b trainers

  c scorers

  d judges.

(1 mark)

3 What is the difference between a player and a performer?

(2 marks)

21. Organisation influences

The following organisations all work to increase opportunities for people to participate in physical activity.

Sport England

Revised

This is a government agency that provides funding and facilities, measures participation and identifies priority groups. It has the overall aim of increasing the number of people who play sports regularly and reducing the number of young people who stop playing sport when they finish school.

Funding

Sport England receives a vast amount of money to distribute to various organisations and projects (over £1 billion between 2012 and 2017). The following are some of the main recipients:

- County Sports Partnerships
- National governing body work
- Facility development
- Schools – to help with school games and access to education facilities, including protecting school playing fields
- Community sport developments

Facilities

Funding is provided through an application process to transform the places where people play sport. Funding is available for the following:

- **'Iconic facilities'** – these tend to be the really big multi-sport facilities; the idea here is that improving these sorts of facilities could very significantly increase the number of participants.
- **'Inspired facilities'** – this funding makes it easier for local community and volunteer groups to improve and refurbish their sports clubs or turn non-sporting venues into modern sporting venues. Help is given with planning these, especially in terms of the design.
- **Protecting playing fields** – in the past, schools have sold playing field land in order to raise money; the aim of this funding is to help schools keep their playing fields and to improve them as well.

Measuring participation

Sport England carries out research to find out whether its funding is having the hoped-for result – increasing participation in sport.

The Active People Survey is used to measure this and each year the data is published the 'Sports Facts' document.

Identifying priority groups

Sport England also aims to increase participation in particular priority groups, such as disabled people and young people.

National governing bodies

Revised

These provide and support the following:

- **Coaching** – each governing body provides the specific training for coaches for their sport. This is provided at various levels, working right up to national and international level. A charity called Sports Coach UK has been formed to work with the national governing bodies to help to recruit, develop and retain coaches.

- **Officiating** – the governing bodies are responsible for setting and interpreting the rules/regulations for their sport so part of this is also to train and provide officials. In a similar way to coaching, this is carried out at various levels according to the different standards and provisions of each sport.

- **Talent development** – every sport wants to be as successful as possible and identifying and developing the talent of the future is one way in which this can be achieved. An organisation known as UK Sport has formed the UK Talent Team to help the national governing bodies with talent development. Once a talented performer has been identified they are linked to the appropriate governing body for coaching support.

- **Competitions** – these are arranged at all levels of sport, from school through to international, to allow the competitors to develop as fully as possible and progress to the highest possible standard.

Youth Sport Trust

Revised

The aim of the Youth Sport Trust is 'To change young people's lives through sport to: give each child a sporting start in life through high quality PE and sport in primary schools; ensure all young people have a sporting chance by developing opportunities for those with special educational needs and disabilities; and support all young people to achieve their sporting best in school and their personal best in life.'

Managing school sport competition

The major schools sport competition run by the Youth Sport Trust is the national School Games (sponsored by Sainsbury's, the supermarket chain), which was first held in 2012. There are four levels to the games, starting in schools, between schools, at county/area level, and finally up to the national finals event.

Leadership and volunteering programmes

Sport relies on over 1.5 million volunteers, officials, coaches, administrators and managers and examples of the Youth Sport Trust's programmes currently (2014) include:

- Lead 2014
- Learning leaders
- Young Ambassadors
- Volunteering in School Sport (School Organising Crews/Committees)
- Leadership Academy

Exam tip

The exam board has stated that students taking the exam should know about any two of these leadership and volunteering programmes, or similar programmes that have since replaced them.

Programmes to engage young people in PE and sport

Revised

Examples of these include:

- Bikeability
- Bupa Start to Move
- Change4Life Sports Clubs
- Fit for Girls
- Matalan yoUR Activity
- Premier League for Sport
- Project Ability
- School Sport Clubs
- TOP Sportsability

Exam tip

The exam board has stated that students taking the exam should only know about any two of these programmes to engage young people in PE and sport, or similar programmes that have since replaced them.

Exam tip

The exam board has stated that the programmes relating to leadership and volunteering and engagement programmes are likely to change over time so any relevant responses will be accepted. It is recommended that the following website is checked regularly: www.youthsporttrust.org/how-we-can-help/programmes.aspx

Dame Kelly Holmes Legacy Trust

Revised

The aim of the trust is to 'get young lives on track by providing support from world class sports stars'. Since 2008 the Trust has helped over 100 world-class athletes to further their careers. The two main aims are to:

1 inspire participation
2 mentor young people.

The main Trust charity projects currently underway are:

- Get on Track
- London 2012 Young Leaders Programme
- AQA Unlocking Potential
- National Citizen Service
- Sport for Change
- Aspiring Minds
- Sporting Champions
- Young People Re-engagement Programme.

Exam tip

The exam board has stated that students taking the exam should only know about any two of these DKHLT projects. They have also noted that these may change over time so any relevant responses will be credited. They also recommend checking the following website for updated information: http://dkhlegacytrust.org/Charity-Projects

1 Sport England aims to increase participation in sport through all of the following except:

   a   funding

   b   managing school sport competitions

   c   facilities

   d   measuring participation. *(1 mark)*

2 National governing bodies aim to provide and support all of the following except:

   a   coaching

   b   officiating

   c   sponsoring

   d   talent development. *(1 mark)*

3 All of the following are projects run by the Youth Sport Trust except:

   a   Get on Track

   b   Lead 2014

   c   The School Games

   d   Young Ambassadors. *(1 mark)*

4 All of the following are projects run by the Dame Kelly Holmes Legacy Trust except:

   a   Aspiring Minds

   b   Fit for Girls

   c   Sporting Champions

   d   Sport for Change. *(1 mark)*

22. International sport

There are many international sporting events which are regularly organised. For any sports performer their ultimate aim is to compete at international level both for themselves and their countries.

Each sport also aims to increase its profile by organising and arranging world cups or world championships for their own particular sport – some sports have even arranged different competitions for the different formats which exist in their game.

World cups/championships   Revised ☐

The highest profile world cups/championships include:

- **The football World Cup** – this is played for the Jules Rimet Trophy. First played in 1930, this is just about the oldest organised world cup. Many other sports have followed the organisation and model of the football World Cup due to its very high international appeal and success. As is the case with many of these championships, it is held every four years. Just about every country in the world plays football and has an international football team. Therefore the entry for the competition is huge and qualifying competitions have to be held.

- **Rugby** – the Rugby World Cup was first competed for in 1987 and is also held every four years. There are not as many rugby-playing nations in the world so, although there are qualifying competitions, the event is not yet as high profile as the football version.

- **Cricket** – the majority of high profile international cricket is played using the five-day test match format between the major cricket playing nations. A ranking system has been introduced to add the incentive of becoming the number one ranked nation. Cricket has different formats so it has a World Cup for its one-day format (first played for in 1975) and a World Twenty20 competition, which was first played for in 2007. The one-day format version is played for every four years and the Twenty20 version every two years.

- **Athletics** – the first World Championship was only started in 1991 and also takes place every four years, two years apart from every Olympic Games.

High profile events   Revised ☐

It is not just world cups and world championships that make up the most important international events. There are others linked to specific sports as well:

- **Wimbledon** – there is no particular world championship for tennis. There are Grand Slam tournaments (Wimbledon, the French Open, Australian Open and American Open) that are played for every year. There is also a ranking system to decide which player is the world number one.

- **Golf** – in a similar way to tennis, golf has four Majors (the British Open, American Open, Masters and PGA Championship) which are the most sought-after wins for players. The Ryder Cup (between the European and American teams) has now also become a very high profile event.

- **American Football Superbowl** – this is the most watched US television broadcast and also has high viewing figures throughout the world. It is called a world championship but only American teams are eligible!

- **Football leagues** – these are very high profile throughout the world and each country has its own 'pyramid' (lower leagues at the bottom, the highest 'premier' one at the top) and version of the Premiership, as the English league has.

- **One-off events** – many sports, such as boxing in particular, arrange these for high profile performers within their particular sport.

Exam tip

The examiner is likely to ask questions specifically regarding why these events are held and what the advantages and disadvantages are to the sports and to the host venues – see below.

Hosting – advantages and disadvantages

Revised

Many continents, countries and cities are keen to host one of these major events. Because of this, many of the sports have a bidding system allowing hosts to come forward and be selected.

Advantages

The main perceived advantages are:

- making a large financial profit
- a raised national/international profile and therefore status
- provision of brand-new or updated facilities – commonly referred to as the 'legacy' –which are available for general use after the event has been held.

Disadvantages

The main perceived disadvantages are:

- security issues and the threat of terrorism attacks
- possible boycotts and political intervention issues
- high costs for the staging and security, with no guarantee of recovering these.

Check your understanding

Tested

1 All of the following sports have organised world cups except for:

   a football

   b cricket

   c rugby

   d tennis. *(1 mark)*

2 All of the following are Grand Slam tennis tournaments except:

   a the US Open

   b the Masters

   c the French Open

   d Wimbledon. *(1 mark)*

3 Describe three advantages to be gained from hosting a major international sporting event. *(3 marks)*

23. The Olympic Games

The Olympic Games is easily the highest profile major international event and competition. First held in 776 BC in Olympia, the Games properly got underway in 1896 when they were held in Greece as a tribute to the 776 BC original.

The various Games hosted in different eras provide good examples of the advantages and disadvantages associated with being the host nation or city.

Previous games   Revised ☐

Berlin 1936

These Games were used by Adolf Hitler as a propaganda campaign to promote his political beliefs. Both Hitler and the Nazi party he led had extreme racist views with regard to Jews and black people. The fact that a black American athlete, Jesse Owens, won four gold medals was an embarrassment for Hitler and the Nazis.

Munich 1972

These Games were marred by an attack led by Palestinian terrorists against Israeli athletes. Hostages were held and, when the siege came to an end, eleven of the hostages were killed along with one police officer and five of the terrorists.

This was the first incident of terrorism at the Olympic Games and the need to provide very high levels of security for high profile events stems from this time.

Montreal 1976

At this time South Africa had the policy of **apartheid** in place (this existed from 1964 until 1990). Montreal was the first Games that some countries chose not to attend (called boycotting) to make a political point. In total, 30 nations refused to send teams in protest at the apartheid system. South Africa was later banned from participating in the Games; this ban was lifted in 1992.

There was another major problem with the Montreal Games: Montreal as host city suffered a huge overall loss of revenue. It meant they were still repaying the debt 30 years later!

> **Key term**
>
> **Apartheid** – a policy of separating groups, especially because of race or colour

Moscow 1980

This was another Games affected by boycotts because the USA refused to send their team in protest about the Soviet invasion of Afghanistan. The Great Britain team was 'advised' not to go so some athletes did attend and some did not. In total, 52 nations boycotted the Games, which seriously reduced the standard of competition.

Los Angeles 1984

The Los Angeles Games proved to be a major turning point for another reason – this was the first Games to make a large 'surplus' (technically

the International Olympic Committee (IOC) does not accept a 'profit')
due to the high levels of sponsorship and commercialism which the hosts
managed to negotiate. This prompted greater interest in hosting such
high profile international sporting events, as, for the first time, TV rights,
sponsorship, tourism, ticket sales and marketing were shown to be a real
benefit for the hosts.

London 2012

London was selected to host the Games in 2005 (this is how far in
advance host cities are chosen) and became the first venue to be used
three times: the 1908 and 1948 Games were also held there.

The 'legacy' was a central theme for these Games as the various venues
were selected to redevelop previously rundown areas of London.
A commitment was made to ensure that all the brand-new, state-of-
the-art facilities would be fully used, managed and maintained after the
Games had finished. The 'surplus' made from being the hosts financed
these facilities – without the Games there would not have been the
development or the provision of the facilities.

These Games also highlighted another benefit of being hosts – that of
greater success for home performers! This was the most successful Games
in modern times for the GB team, something which was partly put down
to home advantage.

> **Exam tip**
>
> The examiner will not ask any
> questions about specific Olympic
> Games or problems associated with
> them. However, knowing about
> these examples and the associated
> advantages and disadvantages
> provides good information for
> answers relating to high profile
> events.

Check your understanding
Tested

1 The gap between a host successfully bidding for the Olympic Games and staging them
  is:

  a 4 years

  b 5 years

  c 6 years

  d 7 years.   (1 mark)

2 The Games which first suffered from an act of terrorism was:

  a Berlin

  b Montreal

  c Munich

  d Moscow.   (1 mark)

3 All of the following are disadvantages of staging the Games except:

  a being unable to attract sponsorship

  b high security costs

  c possible financial losses

  d threats of boycotts.   (1 mark)

24. Competitions

All sports are competitive and all have their own arrangements for the various competitions which best suit their sport.

Competition formats   Revised

Leagues

This is one of the most common forms of competition. Teams are put into various leagues and all teams, or players, play against each other. Games/matches are usually played at home and away and there is a promotion and relegation system whereby bottom teams go down a level and top teams are promoted to a higher league.

- **Advantages** – guaranteed number of games; advance notice of all games and fixtures; the most profitable format for many professional sports; can cater for large numbers of entries with as many leagues as necessary.
- **Disadvantages** – can take a long time to be played if each team has to play each other twice; a lower league team can take many years to reach a higher league; fixture cancellations (possibly due to bad weather) can lead to fixture congestion at the end of a sporting season.

Knockouts

These are played in various rounds where two teams, or individuals, play against each other and the winners go through to the next round until there are only two teams/individuals left to contest the final. Some knockout competitions have preliminary rounds to ensure there is the correct number to take part; for example, 64 starting teams or players are reduced to 32, 16, 8, 4 and then 2 for the final. Knockouts often use a **seeding** format to allow the highest ranked teams automatic entry to the final stages.

- **Advantages** – very quick and relatively easy to organise; can be played over a fairly short time period; can cater for large numbers as half are eliminated after each round.
- **Disadvantages** – a team/player could play only one game/match; qualifying rounds might need to be set up in order to get down to a manageable number.

> **Key term**
>
> **Seeding** – the best players or teams are chosen/selected to automatically qualify and be kept apart in early rounds

Ladders

A set number of players all have their names down on a list (ladder) and they have to challenge the players above them on the ladder in order to take their place if they win. This is a very common format for many racket sports such as tennis, squash and badminton. There are often rules about how many places above you are able to challenge so it is not possible to move straight from the bottom to the top.

- **Advantages** – very well suited to some sports which have individual competitors; very simple and easy to run and administer; can be on-going with no time restrictions; competition is very even with similar standard players.

- **Disadvantages** – progress can be very slow; the entry number is quite restricted as this would not suit a very large entry; unsuitable for team events.

Round robin

In this format all the players, or teams, play against each other – usually only once.

- **Advantages** – a guaranteed number of games; all players/teams get to play against each other; one loss does not mean exclusion from the competition.
- **Disadvantages** – only really suitable for small entry numbers as so many games have to be played; only really suitable for certain sports – tennis being the most notable one.

Combination events

These combine elements of all the forms of competition outlined above. They are very common in international competition as it is possible to play leagues as a qualifying method and then progress to a knockout stage as the competition reaches its final. The football and rugby World Cups use this format.

- **Advantages** – very large numbers/entries can be accommodated; no limit to entry numbers; in the early stages one loss does not mean elimination.
- **Disadvantages** – can take a long time to complete (football and rugby World Cups take three years); teams can qualify early in the initial league stage, leading to some pointless fixtures.

> **Exam tip**
>
> The examiner is likely to ask which format is most suitable for a specific type of sport or entry. You should also link this to the advantages and disadvantages of any chosen format.

Check your understanding   Tested

1 The following are all advantages of the league format except:

   a there is no overall time restriction

   b can cater for a large entry

   c ensures everyone has the same number of games

   d arrangements and fixtures can be set well in advance. ⸱   *(1 mark)*

2 The knockout is a common competition format in some sports. Using an example, explain how the knockout format works.   *(4 marks)*

25. The media and media influences

The media includes all the forms of mass communication which exist. The media makes a very important contribution in helping to give an understanding of sporting performance and participation.

Television   Revised ☐

There are different types both of coverage and ways in which television is broadcast.

- **Coverage** – this includes live sporting programmes; highlights programmes; documentaries; quiz programmes; news bulletins; dedicated club channels (major sports such as football); specific schools programmes; skill development and instructional series; coaching series; magazine programmes; text information; interactive services offering alternative commentaries/views/action/information or events and competitions.

- **Types** – there are three main types of broadcast:
  - **Digital terrestrial television** – these are the main TV providers whose broadcasts can be accessed via a TV set with an aerial. In the UK these are BBC, ITV, Channel 4 and Channel 5.
  - **Satellite and digital broadcasters** – in the UK the main broadcaster is Sky Television (with a whole set of dedicated sports channels) but there is also BT Sport, Virgin Media, ESPN and Eurosport. The satellite broadcast also offers many other features such as 'catch-up', 'any time' and interactive options within each channel choice.
  - **Computer/internet access** – both terrestrial and satellite providers offer access to their programmes via the internet. This means viewers can watch sports coverage on computers, laptops, tablets and mobile phones via broadband internet.

↑ *Soccer Saturday* – one of Sky Sports' most popular broadcasts

Radio

Revised

Developments in radio broadcasting have led to a big increase in the number of sports broadcasts. There are terrestrial broadcasters that broadcast on FM, AM and long- and medium-wave networks. There are also digital radio broadcasts which can be accessed through computers, satellite TV, mobile devices and DAB radios.

Radio broadcasters are able to provide most of the same services as TV providers can (except for actual pictures), but they have the advantage of cheaper broadcasting costs (so companies can afford to cover more sports and fixtures). They also have the benefit of very wide access, as people can listen to radios in their cars and (thanks to radio on mobile phones) virtually anywhere they go.

The press

Revised

This includes the following:

- **Newspapers** – these are printed and available daily (usually morning editions but some evening editions too) and sport is always a major feature. It is traditional for sport to be featured at the back of each edition and there are usually sports 'supplements' in Saturday and Sunday editions. The major newspapers now make their daily editions available digitally to be accessed on mobile devices, laptops and computers.

- **Magazines** – general magazines often have specific sports sections but there are also magazines linked to specific sports or activities, or to targeted readerships such as young males or females.

- **Books** – these can vary from educational textbooks (such as this one!), coaching/instructional books, sporting autobiographies, rule books and sport-specific books. These are available either in hard copy or digitally via e-readers.

The internet

Revised

All of the forms of the media mentioned above can be accessed online. The internet also offers additional functions:

- **Search engines** – these allow information to be accessed, such as general information like facts and figures, and can also be used to search for sports-related websites.

- **Websites** – every sport and physical activity has many websites relating to it, and all sports associations and governing bodies have their own websites. These provide an enormous range of information, opinion and discussion about every aspect of performance and participation in sport.

- **Social networking** – the use of Facebook and Twitter allows up-to-date information and views to be shared, both about sport as a spectator and about ways to participate in sport and physical activity.

> **Exam tip**
>
> The examiner is likely to ask questions regarding the types of media which exist, linked to the types of output they are responsible for.

Media influences

The media is very influential in shaping views and opinions about performance and participation.

Positive influences

- **Information provision and updating** – the media allows everyone to be kept up to date and informed. Both instruction and entertainment can be included. This can increase both support and participation by keeping individuals informed about what and where sport is occurring.

- **Educational uses** – TV companies provide school-level programmes on sport, coaching and skill development. This allows greater access for all learners.

- **Variety of content** – the media is able to provide a huge range of provision and output.

- **Demonstrating performance** – the visual aspect of television in particular enables high standards of performances to be visible, while the use of technology **such as slow-motion and action replays** allow these to be analysed in detail. Televisions (and computers) allow CDs, DVDs and hard drive recordings to be used and replayed.

- **Revenue source** – TV, and satellite TV in particular, pay large amounts of money to be able to provide coverage of major sporting events. They often bid against each other and negotiate with the organisers (or specific clubs or sports) to decide the amounts they are willing to pay for 'exclusive coverage'. TV companies even pay for the privilege of being able to broadcast highlights programmes and the money they pay goes directly to the sports involved.

- **Links to sponsors** – companies sponsor sport in order to get more media attention for their products and services. The greater the media attention, the more sponsors will pay for it, which brings more money into the sport concerned (see topic 26 for more details).

- **Technological advances** – TV companies have developed new techniques to aid their sports coverage, especially in regard to checking officials' decisions; **for example, tracking ball flights and impact points.** These technological advances have often then been adopted by the sports to help officials make correct decisions and allow participants the option of reviewing decisions made by the officials. (See topic 31 for more details.)

Negative influences

- **Media pressure** – if the media decide to mount campaigns against a performer or team then this can be damaging for performance. **For example, media pressure has led to managers and coaches being forced to resign their posts.**

- **TV directors' influence** – directors of a TV broadcast can decide what events or sports are seen or highlighted. They can even decide what is to be said about the event or sport, in terms of comments as commentary or summary discussions. This also applies in the written media where opinions can be stated and justified.

> **Exam tip**
>
> Make sure you know about media influences on performance and participation, both positive and negative. It would be useful to be able to give an example of both a positive and a negative influence.

- **Popularity** – if a sport is given a high media profile (this usually applies to TV in particular) then it is likely to become more popular. This has been the case with both darts and snooker in recent years. Conversely, if a sport is not featured it is less likely to have high levels of participation and support.

- **Levels of support** – spectators may decide that it is an easier and cheaper option to watch an event on TV rather than attend in person. The supporters are still supporting, but the club or organisation doesn't get the revenue from ticket sales, which can have a negative impact on their finances.

- **Undermining officials** – big screens and replays at sports grounds can show an incorrect decision, bad tackle, off-the-ball incident or foul play which the officials missed and can even cause crowd unrest and poor behaviour.

- **Altered event timings** – many organisers are so closely linked to the media supporting their event that they are willing to change the start times and even dates to accommodate them. **For example, the National Football League for American football requires twenty 'television timeouts' per game in order for TV commercials to be shown.**

- **Intrusion** – at any event there may be a great many photographers, reporters, cameramen, sound technicians, cables, gantries and scaffolding, all of which can get in the way of the paying spectators or even distract the players.

Check your understanding

Tested

1 All of the following are examples of the media except:

   a television

   b radio

   c sponsors

   d the press. *(1 mark)*

2 Television programmes include all the following except:

   a documentaries

   b quiz programmes

   c coaching series

   d search engines. *(1 mark)*

3 Describe one positive and one negative influence a director of a live TV sports broadcast could have on viewers' enjoyment of a broadcast. *(4 marks)*

26. Sponsorship and sponsorship influences

Sponsorship and its influence is closely linked to the media and its influence (see topic 25).

Sponsorship – range and scope
Revised

Sponsorship has an effect on sport at just about all levels.

Specific sports and competitions

Many sports arrange and negotiate sponsorship deals and the sponsors like the opportunity to be associated with a high profile and successful sport. **For example, in professional football, the Premier League has one sponsor, the Football League has another, and the two major cup competitions (FA Cup and League Cup) also have sponsors.**

Teams and events

Both national teams and major clubs have their own sponsors – because this is the highest level of sport there is usually no shortage of companies and organisations willing to pay for this privilege. There will be a great number of willing sponsors for many high profile international events. **For example, for the London Olympic Games in 2012, Adidas sponsored the Great Britain team and supplied kit (this caused a clash with Nike who had individual kit deals with athletes) while Coca-Cola was the main event sponsor.**

Every Premier League and Football League club has a sponsor logo on their team shirt and this can vary from year to year. Many of these clubs are now having their venues or stadiums renamed according to the sponsor. **For example, the Oval cricket ground has changed its name four times in recent years from The Kennington to The Fosters to The Brit and then The Kia Oval in December 2010 for a deal worth £3.5 million over a five-year period.**

← Mo Farah in his Adidas 2012 kit – he normally wears rival sponsor Nike kit!

Individuals

Every high profile sports performer is able to negotiate their own personal sponsorship. The higher the profile of the performer, the greater the amount of the sponsorship. **For example, after he became the world number one golfer in 2012, Rory McIlroy signed a ten-year deal with Nike which guaranteed him £155 million (which works out at £42,000 a day). In 1999 David Beckham signed a lifetime deal with Adidas worth £100 million.** However, these huge deals are only available for the highest profile performers. It is much more difficult to obtain sponsorship for lower profile sports and performers.

Acceptability of sponsorship

Revised

Not all companies or brands are acceptable to the authorities who set the rules for specific sports. Tobacco and any smoking products have now been banned for many years – they were once prominent in many sports.

Alcoholic drinks are not acceptable in some sports; this is particularly the case if the sports are particularly associated with younger performers.

Some foods, and some fast food chains, have been deemed unacceptable due to disputes over the nutritional value of the products. This controversy has even spilled over to some drinks manufacturers who have made efforts to reduce sugar levels in their products as a result.

Recently there has been controversy about financial loan companies and betting firms as some people think these companies encourage people to get into debt or to waste money they need for more important things. **For example, Newcastle footballer Papiss Cissé objected to wearing his club shirt advertising Wonga (a loan company) for this reason.** Also, some performers have refused to wear the advertising logos (or blacked them out) on religious grounds.

Types of sponsorship

Revised

- **Money payments** – this is the most common form of sponsorship. It involves the sponsors paying an agreed fee in return for which the individual/club/team joins in advertising campaigns for the sponsor's product and regularly uses the product.

- **Equipment** – the sponsor provides all the equipment a performer needs, usually the brand of the sponsor. Some brands even design and promote a range of equipment using the performer's name.

- **Clothing** – as with equipment, all the performer's clothing and footwear is provided so that the brand name is given a high profile. This is one of the most competitive areas of sponsorship because of the size of the sports clothing and footwear industry.

- **Accessories** – performers are paid to wear items ranging from watches (worn by tennis players, often on the serving-arm wrist so that it is seen by cameras) to sunglasses (standard for cricketers) and hats. Performers even negotiate deals for what they wear and promote when not playing – such as aftershaves or perfumes.

- **Transport and travel** – this can range from having a free car provided to being flown to different events by particular airlines. Even at lower levels, coach companies may arrange sponsorship deals.

- **Training** – assistance with training is provided, sometimes by subsidising time off work to train (for many amateur performers) or providing the equipment or facilities to allow the training to take place. Coaches and trainers can be provided and paid for by the sponsors.

- **Entry fees and expenses** – these can mount up and accommodation in particular can be very expensive if a lot of travel is involved. Many performers have negotiated deals with particular hotel chains.

- **Food** – sometimes a particular type of food is important, which can also provide a sponsorship opportunity.

Not all of these levels of sponsorship are available to all performers. Once again, it is linked to the profile of the performer. A very successful professional is likely to get more sponsorship opportunities than a low-level amateur.

> **Exam tip**
>
> The examiner is likely to ask a question regarding the ease of obtaining sponsorship at different levels. This may also be linked to what type of sponsorship this is most likely be.

Benefits to the sponsors

Revised

- **Advertising** – this is the main benefit for sponsors. They have large advertising budgets and, since a great deal of sport is covered by the media (see topic 25), especially television, sponsorship is a good way of getting a company's product seen by millions of people. The advertising serves to increase sales and therefore profits for the company.

- **Image** – sport has a healthy, successful, positive image and it is a benefit for a company to be able to associate itself and its products with this image. The company also gains goodwill from helping out the sport, which helps to improve its image.

- **Tax relief** – companies are allowed to claim back a certain amount of the money they provide for sponsorship against the taxes they have to pay.

- **Research and development** – new products are tried out by the top level performers to see how well they work.

Advantages and disadvantages of sponsorship to sport

Revised

Advantages

- A lucrative sponsorship deal can allow the performer to concentrate on their sport. They can focus on training and then performing, without any financial worries.

- Specific sports can be promoted, developed and become more successful.

- Competitions can be bigger and better, often with much higher levels of prize money being available.

- Both the profile and image of a sport can be raised and improved.

Disadvantages

- Dates can be changed to suit demands from sponsors – the start time of major events, in particular, will be arranged to coincide with peak-time television viewing. This can affect international sport, with the associated problems of time-zone differences around the world.

- Clothing/equipment restrictions – the type of clothing worn, or equipment used, may not always be the most suitable for the performer but they have to use it nonetheless.

- Withdrawal of sponsorship – sponsors are very sensitive about image and sponsorship deals can be withdrawn from performers if they are associated with anything bad. Having to maintain a 'squeaky clean' public image can add to the pressure on high profile performers, and sudden collapses in sponsorship deals can make it difficult to maintain performance standards.

- Inequality – minority sports can find it very difficult to obtain any level of sponsorship. This is also the case for performers within that minority sport, particularly low level performers.

> **Exam tip**
>
> Make sure you know examples of the main advantages and disadvantages of sponsorship.

Check your understanding
Tested

1 All of the following would be acceptable forms of sponsorship in the UK except:

   a clothing firms

   b sunglasses manufacturers

   c cigarette brands

   d soft drinks companies.   (1 mark)

2 All of the following are advantages of sponsorship except:

   a equipment restrictions

   b sport profile promotion

   c ease of financial worries

   d good image promotion.   (1 mark)

3 Describe why the profile level of a performer may affect their levels of sponsorship.   (4 marks)

27. Role models

A role model is a person whose behaviour, example or success is, or can be, copied by others – particularly younger people. People look up to them and are encouraged to be like them.

Impact of role models

The main effects of sporting role models are as follows:

- **Setting participation trends** – if a role model achieves success in a particular sport or activity then more young people are likely to want to participate in that sport. This can be either general or specific. **For example, role models in football encourage young people to play football (specific); disabled role models have resulted in greater levels of participation in all aspects of disabled sport provision (general).**

← **Paralympian David Weir with his London 2012 gold medals**

- **Shaping attitudes** – there is a great deal of responsibility placed on a role model as the attitudes they help to shape must be positive ones. They have to be seen to compete fairly and by the rules, and they have to be a good performer in their own right and therefore become successful and famous through this. The increasing media scrutiny they are under means that they have to conduct themselves well in both their private and public lives. Because of their very public role, they may have to sacrifice a degree of privacy.

- **Influence on growth** – if a sport or activity is lucky enough to have one or more good role models associated with it, a likely result is a growth of interest and then participation, either in terms of supporters/spectators or actual performers/players.

- **Declining popularity** – if a sport has a clear lack of role models, it is less likely to be able to either gain or maintain its popularity. An even worse situation can arise if someone is seen to be a poor role model as this can result in people being put off a particular sport.

> **Exam tip**
>
> Make sure you are clear on ways in which role models can help set participation trends or shape attitudes. Being able to give examples of current good role models will help with these answers.

Role model pressure

Role models sometimes enjoy a great deal of fame and wealth. This can come at a price and there are many examples of role models who have found it difficult to maintain the high standards expected from them.

● **Media pressure** – the link these role models have with the media means that they are always in the public eye and can lead to a lack of privacy.

● **Competition for their endorsement** – a particularly high profile performer may have several manufacturers or companies trying to work with them. The performer needs to take care not to select a company whose image, and possibly products, do not live up to some public expectations.

● **Being targeted by other performers** – this also includes anyone who seeks to ruin or damage their reputation because of envy.

● **Effects on performance** – pressure outside of their sport can lead to a decline in performance; they may have training schedules interrupted or find the pressures of expectation too great.

● **Managing change** – when their sporting careers come to a close, it can be difficult for role models to make the transition to a new career in which they have a much lower public profile – and a much smaller wage packet!

Check your understanding

1 All of the following are positive effects role models can have except:

   a   setting participation trends

   b   setting an example for others to follow

   c   shaping attitudes

   d   ignoring etiquette expectations.   *(1 mark)*

2 All of the following can be a negative effect due to pressure on a role model except:

   a   lack of privacy

   b   greater financial gain

   c   possible performance decline

   d   endorsing unsuitable products.   *(1 mark)*

3 Choose a sports personality who is a positive role model and explain how they have made a particular activity more popular.   *(4 marks)*

28. Health and safety

Safety precautions must always be in place to ensure the wellbeing of others. Legislation works to make sure this happens and all players must be aware of the potential hazards of taking part in any form of physical activity.

Play safe
Revised

This is a series of health and safety guidance and legislation produced for all physical activities. It sets out the basic rules which need to be applied.

Environment
Revised

The environment is relevant to health and safety concerns:

● **The weather** – if the temperature is very low then outdoor areas may be frozen and unplayable. If it is very high then the ground may be too hard for certain activities and high temperatures could result in sunburn/sunstroke or dehydration. It is not possible to play certain sports if there are thunderstorms – for example, golf.

● **Playing areas** – these need to be carefully checked to make sure they are safe. Outdoor areas could have dangerous objects such as glass, stones, damaged fencing, uneven surfaces or protruding post sockets. Indoor areas may have slippery floors or equipment that has not been put away or stored properly.

Equipment
Revised

Equipment is important for keeping players/performers safe:

● **Playing equipment** – performers should always use the correct equipment for the activity being performed. Safety helmets are appropriate for cricket but not for rugby! Equipment must also be worn correctly, with laces done up and any loose straps tucked away. Checks should also be made to ensure that the equipment is in good condition and good working order – splinters from damaged hockey sticks or rounders bats can be dangerous. Large pieces of equipment such as soccer, hockey and rugby posts must be checked to see if they are safe and in some cases (rugby) have protective surrounds added.

● **Footwear/clothing** – many sports have their own specific protective clothing – shin pads must be worn by all footballers and gum shields are recommended for rugby and hockey. Hockey goalkeepers and cricket batters have a large range of additional safety equipment to wear. Many activities have rules that ensure this safety equipment is used and worn at all times. Footwear also needs to be correct and appropriate; certain surfaces require particular footwear to be worn, such as studded boots for rugby and football, and checks need to be made to ensure that these studs are in good order with no sharp, dangerous edges. Footwear needs to give support to arches and to cushion the impact on the ankle joint when running and jumping.

> **Exam tip**
>
> The examiner is likely to ask questions relating to why health and safety is important. You will also need to give specific examples of how it can help to prevent injury.

Prior preparation

This includes all aspects of preparing to take part, including:

- **training to the correct level to be able to take part** – for example, you would not take part in a marathon without undertaking a great deal of training preparation beforehand

- **warming up and then cooling down as part of every practical session** – both training and performing

- **correct physical state** – this includes:

    - removing all items of jewellery and even making sure that fingernails are kept short if playing netball (this is checked by the officials)

    - tying hair back and putting on the correct clothing and equipment, as well as being well aware of the rules so that you are not a danger to yourself or others

    - making sure that any equipment being worn has been washed and cleaned.

Participation during a performance

When a performance is actually underway, the following applies:

- The correct actions using the correct techniques must be used at all times. **For example, a high tackle in rugby is illegal because it is extremely dangerous, as is a two-footed tackle in football.**

- Officials must be obeyed at all times; this is particularly important in any sports which allow physical contact.

- Balanced and fair competition must be in place – this is why age group categories are used and also why many martial arts and boxing have specified weight categories.

Lifting and carrying

A general rule always applies whenever someone is lifting and/or carrying anything: the knees should be bent and the back kept straight. When any object is being carried it should be kept as close to the body as possible.

Check your understanding

1 All of the following are environmental factors affecting safety except:

  a the weather

  b ground conditions

  c temperature

  d equipment checks. *(1 mark)*

2 All of the following are reasons for wearing the correct footwear except:

  a to ensure the correct grip

  b to protect ankles

  c to increase flexibility

  d to cushion the ankle joint. *(1 mark)*

3 Explain two reasons why it is important to always use the correct techniques and actions when participating in physical activity. *(4 marks)*

29. Rules relating to sport and equipment

Rules make sure that participation in sport is safe for all. There are safety considerations that apply to all of the aspects of practical activity and some examples follow.

Games activities

Revised

Many invasion games, such as rugby, football, netball, basketball and hockey, have very specific equipment/clothing rules which apply. **For example, a footballer wears different footwear on a grass pitch than an Astroturf one, or when playing a five-a-side version in a sports hall or gym**. All footwear needs to fit correctly to prevent blisters (very common in racket sports) and to provide some protection against possible impact.

Rugby has rules in place which make sure that only suitably qualified coaches/teachers can take practical sessions. This ensures that sequences in the games, such as tackles, scrums and line-outs (which allow the lifting of players), are both taught and performed safely.

American football players wear a great deal of protective equipment but there are also rules forbidding them to use their safety helmets dangerously when being tackled, or for defenders to grab the helmet when tackling an opposing player. Safety equipment must be used to safeguard a player and not be used in an offensive way.

Gymnastic activities

Revised

The majority of gymnastic activities require the performer to be barefoot or, sometimes, to wear light gymnastic shoes. **For example, a trampolinist would use this sort of footwear to avoid getting their toes caught in the trampoline bed or the protective matting around the frame. They would also make sure that they wore tight-fitting, rather than loose, clothing for the same reasons. The rules relating to trampolining state that only qualified personnel can take a session and 'spotters' must be used to ensure the trampolinist's safety when they are performing or practising**.

Dance activities

Revised

Different forms of dance require different footwear that is suitable, safe and comfortable. Ballet shoes have padding in the toes to protect the toes during certain actions. Tap-dancing shoes are quite big and bulky, while ballroom-dancing shoes have very shiny, slippery soles to allow smooth sliding moves to be performed – too much grip would be a safety issue here!

> **Exam tip**
> Make sure you know at least one rule relating to safety for each activity area.

Athletic activities

Revised

Spiked running shoes, providing grip to prevent slipping, are common for some running and jumping events, depending on the surface being used. However, a thrower who needs to rotate their body will not want to put a strain on their ankles by having too much grip when turning; for this activity spiked shoes would be dangerous.

All landing areas have specific rules relating to the type of materials used in order to make it safe. Pole-vaults can only take place once the full, inflatable landing area is in place and securely positioned.

Water-based activities

Revised

Rules ensure that qualified lifeguards are present for any water-based activities. It is a legal requirement that they are present at any public swimming facilities.

Outdoor and adventurous activities

Revised

Any 'challenging' environment has a great many rules relating to safety within it. All outdoor and adventurous activities have very detailed guidelines and rules regarding who can be in charge, where activities can take place and what equipment must be used for certain activities. **For example, any form of climbing requires specialist footwear, possible protective gloves, safety ropes and helmets, and additional assistants operating the safety ropes.**

Fitness and health activities

Revised

Clothing rules apply (loose clothing is often not allowed) and equipment cannot be used if someone has not been 'inducted' in its use. For free weights activities a training partner has to be used to help lower, support and remove weights for some movements/exercises. There may even be age-related rules in place for some facilities and equipment.

Check your understanding

Tested

1 All of the following would be safety rules relating to games activities except:

   a   correct footwear soles and grips

   b   correctly fitting footwear

   c   use of correct techniques

   d   qualified lifeguards in attendance.   *(1 mark)*

2 All of the following athletes would be required to wear spiked shoes for their safety except:

   a   hammer throwers

   b   long jumpers

   c   sprinters

   d   pole-vaulters.   *(1 mark)*

3 Describe two examples where a rule exists related to wearing correct footwear.   *(4 marks)*

30. Science in sport

Technology is the practical application of science and in sport this has had a positive effect on both the performance of and involvement in physical activity.

Technological developments
Revised

There are three main areas in which technological developments have had an effect on participation and performance in different activities and for different performers.

Equipment

Developments in technology mean that new manmade materials have often replaced natural materials for equipment. This generally makes the equipment lighter, stronger or more flexible, according to the specific needs of an activity.

- **Racket sports** – all rackets for tennis, badminton and squash were originally made of wood but rackets are now made from carbon-fibre, fibreglass, metal alloys such as titanium, and even ceramics! The strings are now nylon, or polymer-based (for example, polyamide), allowing for much greater tension to be added than could be used before. As the new materials are lighter, it also means that the racket head sizes can be increased without making the rackets any heavier.

- **Pole-vault** – in this event the pole itself has changed dramatically. It was originally made from bamboo or aluminium but now carbon-fibre and fibreglass is used to allow much greater heights to be reached. Because of this, the technology related to the landing areas also needed to be updated. Landing areas are now constructed of partially inflated high tech foam between 3 feet 3 inches (c. 1 metre) to 4 foot 10 inches (c. 1 metre 50 cm) thick. This allows the jumpers to land safely from heights in excess of 20 feet (over 6 metres)!

- **Safety equipment** – many sports, ranging from football to cricket, now make use of lighter, stronger materials which offer greater comfort and improved protection.

Materials

In general, these are the materials which are used for clothing and footwear:

- **Body suits** – these were first worn by swimmers in the 2000 Olympic Games to allow them to be more streamlined and achieve faster times. They proved so successful that they ended up being banned in 2010 because it was felt that some swimmers were gaining an unfair advantage. However, similar versions are still worn by some sprinters and cyclists to reduce the amount of drag or wind resistance.

- **Lighter clothing** – this allows perspiration to disperse easily but still keeps the performer comfortable. This is particularly useful for a marathon runner. At the other extreme, waterproof clothing (for golfers in particular) and better insulated clothing to retain heat have assisted in many outdoor and adventurous activities.

- **Footwear** – this is now very specific for every individual sport, with combinations of natural and synthetic materials making up different part of the shoes or boots. These are generally light, hard wearing, strong and flexible and offer more grip. They are also fully adjustable in terms of lacing-up and can even be partially inflatable to allow a perfect fit.

Facilities

Older, general sports facilities, such as halls and gyms catering for a variety of activities, are not always able to offer the specialised provision which many sports now need. Therefore these now tend to be purpose-built.

- Stadiums are now purpose-built, for example for athletics, rugby and football. Many existing stadiums are being updated and upgraded, with some clubs opting to sell the ones they own in order to move to build new and improved ones. Adding retractable roofs (such as at the Millennium Stadium in Wales and the centre court at Wimbledon) has been possible due to improved technology.

- Sports such as gymnastics have benefitted from specialised facilities. These have allowed better and safer areas to both train and compete; **for example, sprung floors (to enable tumbling) and safety pits beneath the specialist equipment enable the gymnasts to train more effectively.**

- Training equipment available in specialised gyms means that training can now become very focused and specific. This helps to present opportunities for all and not just elite athletes.

> **Exam tip**
>
> Make sure you know how technological innovations have led to improvements in sports performance and participation. It is a good idea to know some specific examples to use in your answers.

Check your understanding | Tested

1 All of the following are technological developments except:

   a fibreglass for pole-vault poles

   b ceramics for rackets

   c polymers for racket strings

   d sports vitamin supplements.   *(1 mark)*

2 Body suits might be worn by cyclists to:

   a match the designs and colours on their bikes

   b keep them drier in wet conditions

   c reduce wind resistance

   d enable more space for advertising logos.   *(1 mark)*

3 Choose one technological development and explain how it has helped to improve performance.   *(4 marks)*

31. ICT in sport

In sport, ICT can be used to:

- record and analyse performance
- improve knowledge and performance.

Recording and analysing performance

There are a great many devices now available that allow performers to record, play back and analyse performances:

- **Video cameras** – this includes standard cameras that also have a video function.

- **Flip-cams** – these often have built-in hard drives to store imagery but use memory cards as well. Replays can be shown on the device itself but can also be played through a laptop or computer via a USB link.

- **Mobile phones** – camera and video camera functions on mobiles have now developed to the point where they are of similar quality to cameras and camcorders. These phones have the added benefit of being able to email or message images to other devices very quickly and easily.

- **Laptops** – these now have integrated cameras and also offer the facility to record and play back action.

- **Tablets** – these have the additional function of apps which can be bought and which can enhance the camera and video functions already on the devices. A commonly used app available on Apple devices (for example, iPhones, iPods and iPads) is known as Coach's Eye.

At the highest levels of sport there are additional devices used, especially for the accurate analysis of achievement:

- **Electronic timing** is used wherever possible and always at top-flight swimming and athletic events. To the human eye it can be difficult to judge positions that are very close, so timing that is accurate to one thousandth of a second is used. In swimming, swimmers touch sensor pads as they finish the race. In athletics the timing devices are also linked to visual imagery and sensors.

- In tennis a device known as **Cyclops** is used to decide if serves are in or out. The machine is specifically calibrated to detect balls which have landed beyond the service line.

- **Hawk-Eye** is a ball-tracking technology used in tennis and cricket, and from August 2013 it was introduced for goal-line technology in football.

  - In tennis this technology is able to accurately track the flight of a ball to tell if a tennis shot is in, on the line or out.

  - In cricket it is used to see the flight a cricket ball would have continued on for LBW decisions.

  - In football it can judge whether a ball crosses the line and therefore whether a goal should be given.

The officials are now able to make use of this technology to ensure that the decisions they make are correct. In both tennis and cricket the players are given opportunities to challenge (in tennis) or review (in cricket) the decisions made.

● Many sports now have **video officials** (or extra officials) who are able to check replays of action, use the technology available and communicate with the officials in charge to either uphold or change decisions.

The technology used to record and analyse performance is advancing at such a rate that even these recent examples are likely to be superseded or replaced quite quickly.

Improving knowledge and performance

Use of the iInternet, interactive tools and devices (and even in some cases games consoles) means that teaching and training aids are now available in abundance. Websites offer a wealth of information and computer programs are constantly being developed.

Data collection and analysis is relatively easily managed. **For example, Prozone is a system used by the majority of football clubs. It provides extremely detailed performance-analysis software tracking the movements of every player on the pitch every tenth of a second and providing information on over 2,500 actions in every match. To do this it makes use of 360-degree camera placement, using a minimum of eight digital cameras at all four corners of the stadium!** This data can then be used to consider the ways in which performances can then be improved.

> **Exam tip**
>
> The examiner is likely to ask questions about the specific forms of ICT which can be used to improve either knowledge or performance.

Check your understanding

Tested

1 Hawk-Eye is currently being used in all of the following sports except:

  a badminton

  b football

  c tennis

  d cricket.   *(1 mark)*

2 All of the following devices can be used for recording and analysing performance except:

  a video cameras

  b tape recorders

  c laptops

  d tablets.   *(1 mark)*

3 Explain why some sports allow the use of ICT technology such as Hawk-Eye. *(4 marks)*

32. Additional Double Award content

This is additional content which must only be covered by students who are taking the Double Award. It is complementary to the Short Course Award and Full Course Award and all of the content in the previous topics needs to be fully covered as well.

Testing components of fitness

This relates specifically to the content covered in topic 14. The specific test(s) for each fitness component is given below:

- **Flexibility** – the sit and reach test which specifically tests the flexibility of the lower back and hamstring muscles
- **Cardiovascular endurance** – the Cooper twelve-minute run and the multi-stage fitness test (also known as the bleep test or continuous shuttle run).
- **Strength** – the hand grip dynamometer which measures the level of forearm muscle strength
- **Agility** – the Illinois agility test
- **Co-ordination** – the alternate hand ball-throw
- **Balance** – the stork stand
- **Power** – the standing broad jump and the vertical jump
- **Reaction time** – the ruler drop test

> **Exam tip**
>
> The examiner is likely to state a component of fitness and ask which particular test is used to measure it. This would be linked to the importance of being able to assess levels of fitness accurately.

Training and preparation

- Applying the knowledge and understanding of the exercise/training programmes in topic 15 – specifically covering the principles of training (topic 16) and linking this to a training session, and a programme, for a named activity and an individual of a specific age.
- Applying the FIT principle (topic 16)
- Preparing performers in skill acquisition and the importance of using the correct technique. This is also linked to being in the correct mental state.
- Skill acquisition – notably:
  - types of skill – to include open skills (such as those which occur in constantly changing situations) and closed skills (such as those which occur in static and unchanging situations)
  - types of guidance – to include visual (seeing a demonstration, an example or watching a playback of your own); verbal (being told what needs to be done, changed or developed) and manual (being physically guided through something, such as a vault support)

- Types of feedback – notably:
  - intrinsic knowledge of performance – something which is sensed or felt by the performer while they are actually performing
  - extrinsic knowledge of results – coming from sources other than the performer themselves, such as the crowd or replays which can be seen
- Types of practice – notably:
  - whole – where a complete performance is carried out in its entirety
  - part – where a specific part of a performance is covered, such as a particular skill
  - fixed – where a particular set session or aspect is concentrated on
  - variable – any combination of the three types above

> **Exam tip**
> The examiner is likely to ask you to link your knowledge to your own personal experiences and practical situations.

Lifestyle choices   Revised ☐

This is covered in three areas.

1 Diet – applying the knowledge and understanding of a balanced diet (topic 17) and the links between exercise, diet, work and rest and the relationship between dietary intake and performance.

2 Activity choices – reasons for choosing different types of activity under the following headings:
  - Enjoyment
  - Company
  - To maintain/improve fitness
  - Relaxation
  - Excitement

3 Appropriate choice of activity, depending on:
  - age (topic 1)
  - physical maturity (topic 1)
  - fitness levels (topic 14)

> **Exam tip**
> The examiner is likely to ask questions linking these lifestyle choices to actual decisions individuals make and the types of activities they choose in particular.

Risk assessment and safe practice   Revised ☐

The following aspects need to be considered in line with having knowledge of being able to apply them in specific situations. This is all linked to topic 28 in particular.

- Safe condition of the environment/playing area – this includes the ability to identify potential risks/hazards in a range of locations/settings, such as playing/performing areas (for example, pitches/courts/gyms/ sports halls/leisure centres/dance studios/swimming pools and various surfaces such as tarmac/grass/artificial indoor and outdoor ones). The appropriate safety checks for all of these should also be known.

- Lifting, carrying and placing equipment safely – being aware that lifting with bent legs and a straight back is important. Handling sports equipment, such as trampolines with the 'wings', needs consideration.

- Correct techniques when performing a skill/activity and/or when landing, including examples of correct and poor techniques and the effect on the performance or outcome. Also the short-term and long-term effects of poor techniques, which could include causing an injury.

- Appropriate clothing and footwear – this includes using protective clothing/footwear and making sure that this is always appropriate for the activity being undertaken.

- The importance of warming up/down in order to prevent injury. This is linked to being able to take a leadership role in a practical session and being aware of all of the following:

  - The effect on body temperature

  - The range of movement increasing

  - The gradual increase of effort to full pace

  - Psychological preparation

  - The practice of movement skills through the whole range of movement

  - Allowing the body to recover, including the removal of lactic acid to prevent soreness/stiffness later

  - Preventing injury

  - Improving performance

- Awareness of the risks involved in any activity and how to minimise them – the safety issues and ways of applying them to arrange of physical activities and events

- Awareness of appropriate safety precautions/rules of a governing body – these will be specific to a particular sport, such as the rule in rugby that only fully qualified rugby specialist should take any teaching sessions.

- First aid and emergency arrangements. This is linked to topic 7 in particular and includes the following:

  - Knowledge of common injuries associated with different activities and actions that should be taken. This could include contact injuries such as bruises, which are common in any physical contact sports, or even blisters on hands and feet, which are associated with many racket sports.

  - Joint and muscle injuries – this includes strains and sprains, pulled muscles and dislocations as well as soft tissue injuries such as cuts and bruises.

  - Recognition of upper/lower limb fractures and the symptoms of concussion, as well as the causes of hypothermia and the actions which have to be taken.

  - The principles of **RICE**, which stands for **R**est, **I**ce, **C**ompression and **E**levation. For Rest the activity must be stopped straight away. Ice should be applied if possible as it reduces swelling and relieves some of the pain, but ice must not be directly applied to the skin – an ice pack is ideal. Compression can be achieved by using a bandage or some tape which gives support to the injured area, but this must not be applied too tightly as it can reduce the blood flow. Elevation can be achieved by raising the injured body part to decrease the circulation and help drain away any other fluids.

For all of these first aid and emergency situations, other points also need to be considered, including:

- how, when and where these injuries happen
- how to avoid all these injuries happening
- what to do if an injury does happen
- the effects on the body.

N.B. It is very important to remember that all of the above is included to make sure that you have knowledge of basic first aid procedures in order to be able to answer a possible question based on it. At no time does this mean that you then have sufficient knowledge for any first aid to be undertaken or carried out!

Due to the large amount of content to be covered in this topic there are no specific 'Check your understanding' examples included. It is likely that this content will be examined specifically through the additional scenario pre-release material, which is part of the additional examination paper.

> **Exam tip**
>
> The examiner is likely to ask specific questions relating to full knowledge of the RICE principle with examples of its effective practical application.

Check your understanding: answers

1. Age and disability (page 7)

1 b *(1 mark)*

2 Answers would get 1 mark for a relevant example and 3 for the explanation, for example: *Age divisions are used because there are physiological factors, which can either be an advantage or a disadvantage for an individual, such as size/strength/ flexibility/experience/skill levels. Examples of age divisions include under fourteen/under sixteen/under eighteen, or year groups at school such as Year 7/10, etc. (4 marks)*

3 Any four of the following for 1 mark each:

- May have physical/health difficulties that limit performance/lack of strength/power/co-ordination/prone to illness
- May have mental/cognitive difficulties that limit performance
- Lack of suitable activities on offer/not many teams available
- Lack of specialist coaches/teachers
- Lack of role models
- Limited access to facilities/no wheelchair access/ no ramps
- Difficulties in transport/getting to facilities
- Limited specialist equipment/resources for disability participation
- Others may discriminate against participation/ getting picked on
- Feeling of helplessness/lack of confidence/low self-esteem/embarrassment
- Lack of money *(4 marks)*

2. Gender and culture (page 9)

1 c *(1 mark)*

2 The general point is in order to make competition fairer. Then three further points from:

- Males tend to be bigger.
- Males tend to be taller.
- Males tend to be stronger.
- Females tend to be more flexible.

- Males do not experience the same level of hormonal imbalances. *(4 marks)*

3 The culture could have a positive effect on participation or a negative one (for 1 mark). Then three further points from:

- A particular culture, influenced by religious views, may not encourage the participation of women.
- A multi-cultural society is likely to welcome full levels of participation by all members of the society.
- Some religions have rules about headwear and clothing which might cause problems for those wishing to participate.
- Some religions may forbid participation at certain times or on certain days.
- Some religions do not consider all sporting activities appropriate for women to take part in. *(4 marks)*

3. Physique and environment (page 11)

1 a *(1 mark)*

2 c *(1 mark)*

3 The general point would be that the weather is likely to have a negative effect (1 mark). You then need another three points, for example:

- An activity could not take place in an outdoor environment if it was too wet (flooded), too cold (frozen), too dry (the surface was too hard to play on); if there were storms (risk of being struck by lightning); if it was too foggy or misty (visibility restricted and therefore dangerous); too windy (ball being blown about and/or dangers to participants to spectators); too dark (bad light stops play in cricket).
- Performers might be affected by becoming too hot (possible dehydration) or too cold (possible hyperthermia). These factors would affect their participation because they might have to stop or slow down, or could lose interest.
- Poor weather, such as lack of snow, would make skiing impossible and lack of wind can make sailing impossible. *(4 marks)*

4. Risk and challenge and activity levels (page 13)

1 a *(1 mark)*

2 Any five of the following:

- Carry out a risk assessment.

- Wear correct clothing/footwear/shoes/properly fastened clothing/well fitting clothing.
- Use personal protective equipment/the right equipment.
- Ensure the activity is supervised/qualified instructor/go with someone else.
- Follow health and safety procedures.
- Check equipment for faults.
- Take the weather/environment/surfaces into account at all times, keep track of where you are and make sure others know where you are.
- Ensure activities are suitable for the age/ability/experience of the participants.
- Lift and carry equipment properly.
- Exercise/compete at an appropriate level/do not overdo it.
- Warm up/cool down appropriately.
- Use the correct skills/techniques.
- Take mobile phones/tell others where you are going.
- Ensure first aid precautions are in place. *(5 marks)*

3 1 mark for the general point initially made and 3 for three examples, which could include:

- Some activities may be too expensive to pay for access/membership/insurance or to obtain equipment/to take part.
- Some activities may not be as acceptable within the particular social circles of an individual or there could be a lack of experience of these activities within the social circles.
- The higher the levels of participation, the more the expense is likely to be, particularly at competitive levels. *(4 marks)*

5. Training (page 15)

1 d *(1 mark)*

2 d *(1 mark)*

3 Two points need to be made, worth 2 marks each, which could include the following:

- They could have the fees waived by the local authority to allow them to use facilities, such as swimming pools, free of charge or they could receive grants towards training costs.
- Amateurs may be able to access additional funding via funding streams such as the National Lottery, which would then allow them to train more regularly. *(4 marks)*

6. Fatigue and stress (page 17)

1 b *(1 mark)*

2 c *(1 mark)*

3 1 mark for a definition – motivation as being the drive to succeed/the desire and energy to achieve something – and 3 for the explanation; for example:

- Stress is likely to raise arousal levels, which will then raise an individual's motivation to succeed. However, if the individual becomes over-aroused it could have the opposite effect and cause them to lose motivation.
- A certain level of anxiety is good and would probably raise motivation levels. However, if there was a great deal of criticism/negative feedback this could be de-motivating and lead to a decrease in performance levels.
- A more introverted personality type is likely to react less positively to stress and therefore lose motivation. *(4 marks)*

7. Injury and safe practice (page 19)

1 1 mark for the activity and 3 for the example:

- In rugby, when tackling, the tackle must not be too high (specifically, the tackle must be made around the legs, never at head height); it is important for the tackler to tuck their head in at the rear of the legs/when the tackle is being made the tackler should grip tightly until the tackle is completed.
- When playing hockey, the hockey stick must not be raised above head height or when other players are close by/the follow-through must be kept low to ensure that other players are not struck by the hockey stick, either from in front or behind. *(4 marks)*

2 1 mark for the activity and 3 for the example:

- In football, shin pads should be worn. This protects the lower front part of the leg in case there is possible impact from another player, as they are specifically designed to protect the shin bone from possible fractures or cuts from another footballer's boots or studs.
- In cricket, batters wear helmets/pads/batting gloves/thigh protectors/arm guards/chest protectors/a box to protect them from being struck by the ball from the bowler or when it is thrown in by fielders. *(4 marks)*

3 d *(1 mark)*

8. Aerobic and anaerobic exercise (page 21)

1 b *(1 mark)*

2 It transports oxygen, glucose and other waste products; it helps with temperature control; it can assist with protection, carrying antibodies and clotting to seal cuts and wounds. *(3 marks)*

3 1 mark for the definition and 3 for three clear explanatory points; for example:
- It is a mild poison and waste product of anaerobic exercise.
- It builds up in the muscles after exercise has finished.
- The most effective way of removing it is to complete a thorough cool-down once the exercise period has been completed. *(4 marks)*

9. The circulatory system (page 23)

1 a *(1 mark)*

2 4 marks for four differences. For example:
- an artery has a thicker wall than a vein
- the vein wall is thinner and less elastic
- veins have valves to make sure that the blood cannot flow backwards
- arteries carry oxygenated blood and veins carry deoxygenated blood. *(4 marks)*

10. Leisure and recreation (page 25)

1 b *(1 mark)*

2 a *(1 mark)*

3 1 mark for each difference:
- Leisure is the free time an individual has/not working or at school/when they have a choice about what they do with their time.
- Recreation is the time to relax/to do something active and healthy. *(2 marks)*

11. Health and fitness (page 27)

1 d *(1 mark)*

2 c *(1 mark)*

3 You need to include three of the four following points for the full 3 marks: a state of complete physical, mental and social wellbeing, and not merely the absence of disease. *(3 marks)*

4. You should make three clear points for the 3 marks; for example, to be able to perform a range of simple movements/without discomfort/such as being able to tie up shoelaces. *(3 marks)*

12. The skeletal system (page 29)

1 a *(1 mark)*

2 b *(1 mark)*

3 c *(1 mark)*

4 For example:
- the shoulder joint, involving the clavicle, scapula and humerus
- the elbow joint, involving the humerus, radius and ulna
- the wrist joint, as it would be bent and allowing the hand to grip the ball. *(3 marks)*

13. The muscular system (page 31)

1 a *(1 mark)*

2 d *(1 mark)*

3 Any two major muscle groups from:
- deltoids
- trapezius
- latissimus dorsi
- pectorals
- biceps
- triceps
- abdominals. *(2 marks)*

4. For 4 marks, state four ways they are kept healthy, for example:
- makes them stronger/bigger
- less likely to strain/injury
- good blood/oxygen supply
- increase tolerance to lactic acid/tire less easily
- can help keep going/helps muscular endurance. *(4 marks)*

14. Fitness components (page 35)

1 b *(1 mark)*

2 d *(1 mark)*

3 a *(1 mark)*

4 For 1 mark, a correct definition as either:
- the ability to produce the correct movement at the optimum time
- the ability to coincide movements in relation to external factors.

Then 3 marks for examples of the advantage; each of these two examples makes three clear points for the 3 marks available.

- Being able to time the service action to hit the ball by combining the throw into the air, taking wind/sun into account/swinging the racket in the opposite direction/making contact with the ball and racket at maximum height.
- Being able to move around the court in relation to where the opponent has placed the ball/to select the appropriate shot (for example, volley, smash, lob, etc.) and then be able to make contact with the ball at the right time in terms of bounce/speed/spin in order to play it into the court. *(4 marks)*

15. Training types and programmes (page 39)

1   220 − 15 = 205 (1 mark for each element of the equation) *(3 marks)*

2   b *(1 mark)*

3   Repetitions are the number of times you perform a particular exercise, such as performing one arm curl. Sets are the number of times you carry out an activity – the total arm curls performed would be one set. *(4 marks)*

4   Your answer should make three clear points, for example:

- To ensure that more time is given for the muscles or muscle groups to recover.
- To avoid tiring those muscles so that they are not able to contract properly/to reduce the effects of fatigue setting in.
- To avoid any possibility of injury/or overuse problems. *(3 marks)*

16. Principles of training (page 41)

1   b *(1 mark)*

2   d *(1 mark)*

3   Each definition is worth 1 mark and each practical example is worth 2 marks:

- Specificity – the training should be particular/relevant/most suited to/most appropriate to needs/relevant energy system used/relevant muscle groups used. For example, choosing main muscle groups used in an activity to train for strength.

- Progression – gradually becoming more difficult/demanding/challenging then, once adapted, making more demands on the body. For example, doing more repetitions of sprints at each training session.
- Overload – work harder than normal/puts body under stress/adaptation will follow/comes about by increasing frequency/intensity/time (duration). For example, lifting heavier weights.
- Reversibility – performance/fitness can deteriorate if training/exercise stops/decreases. For example, if you stop endurance training your stamina levels will reduce in time. *(6 marks)*

17. Diet (page 45)

1   b *(1 mark)*

2   The amount of energy needed/for important processes/such as breathing/keeping the heart beating. *(3 marks)*

3   1 mark for each diet, for example:

a   would suit any type of endurance performer such as a marathon runner

b   this would suit a performer, such as a gymnast or jockey. *(2 marks)*

4   Any two correct reasons, for example:

- to stop the runners becoming dehydrated
- through water loss. *(2 marks)*

18. School influences (page 47)

1   d *(1 mark)*

2   Any two of the following:

- To encourage a healthy, active lifestyle
- To help students acquire and develop skills
- To help students select and apply skills, tactics and compositional ideas
- To help students evaluate and improve performance
- To improve knowledge of fitness and health *(2 marks)*

3   2 marks for the definition – an activity which takes place out of the timetabled lessons, such as pre-school, at lunchtime or after school – and 1 further mark for the example, which could include:

- school team practices
- additional opportunities for clubs such as trampolining or badminton

- trips to outside facilities such as ice skating or ten pin bowling. *(3 marks)*

19. Social and cultural factors (page 51)

1 c *(1 mark)*

2 Your answer should identify both the leisure activity and the target user group, for example, discount swimming sessions for the over-60s. There are many other different examples you could choose. *(2 marks)*

3 1 mark for the definition – etiquette is the unwritten/rules/conventions of an activity – and a further 2 for a suitable example, such as soccer players kicking the ball out of play/to stop the game for an injury to be treated/opponents then returning the ball to their opponents. *(3 marks)*

4 One positive and one negative effect should be given. Here are some examples of both:
   - Positive – can help with transport/equipment/ clothing/provide encouragement/take part with the individual (be a partner or opponent).
   - Negative – can enforce their negative views/ may not be financially able to help/may not have transport or even have time to help with travel. *(4 marks)*

20. Opportunities and pathways (page 53)

1 b *(1 mark)*

2 b *(1 mark)*

3 Your answer should clearly explain the difference:
   - A player takes part in activities which have levels of competitions, teams and opponents.
   - A performer takes part in activities, such as dance and gymnastics, which are more individual and lack a team element. *(2 marks)*

21. Organisation influences (page 57)

1 b *(1 mark)*

2 c *(1 mark)*

3 c *(1 mark)*

4 b *(1 mark)*

22. International sport (page 59)

1 d *(1 mark)*

2 b *(1 mark)*

3 1 mark for each advantage:

- Making a large profit through ticket sales/ sponsorship/media and TV income
- Raising profile/nationally/internationally and encouraging investment/tourism in the area/ improving international reputation/perceptions in other countries
- New/updated facilities are used for the event and therefore available for use afterwards. This also includes improved transport links, housing and accommodation. *(3 marks)*

23. The Olympic Games (page 61)

1 d *(1 mark)*

2 c *(1 mark)*

3 a *(1 mark)*

24. Competitions (page 63)

1 a *(1 mark)*

2 You would get 1 mark for a knockout event – for example, Wimbledon – and 3 marks for the explanation:
   - Qualifying events are often held to decide entries as 128 entries are allowed in the main draw (to be reduced to 64 after the first round) and a world ranking position is also considered.
   - Players are seeded to be kept apart. The number one seed is number one in one half of the draw, and the number two seed is top of the other half of the draw, with all the others evenly spaced out. In theory the number one and two seeds would then meet in the final.
   - The organisers also use a 'wild card' system which grants automatic entry to some players – these are often British competitors or high profile performers who did not qualify via their ranking status. *(4 marks)*

25. The media and media influences (page 67)

1 c *(1 mark)*

2 d *(1 mark)*

3 You should make two developed points for this answer, for example:
   - Positive – can help with understanding/increasing popularity by focusing on good aspects of the play and performance/can choose good action to show and ignore bad aspects such as poor crowd behaviour/can also encourage commentators

and analysts to be positive in their views and comments

- Negative – can look to sensationalise poor but minor incidents such as bad fouls, crowd chants, etc./could look to change start finish times to maximise the viewing figures/can even ask for 'directors' timeouts' for adverts to be broadcast (these occur in American football)/may encourage commentators or analysts to be controversial and even confrontational in interviews, etc. (4 marks)

26. Sponsorship and sponsorship influences (page 71)

1 c *(1 mark)*

2 a *(1 mark)*

3 You need to make two developed points for the full 4 marks. The following examples identify a range of points you could make:

- High level performers attract higher levels of sponsorship/sponsors want to be associated with success/these performers have a higher media profile/they would be seen as role models with more people wanting to emulate them/dress like them, etc.
- Lower level performers do not attract as much media attention as they may not be in a high profile sport which has high media coverage or high attendance at competitions or events. Therefore the sponsors will not get their product seen as widely or have the likelihood of getting sufficient benefits for their investment therefore the sponsors will be concentrating on the high profile options. *(4 marks)*

27. Role models (page 73)

1 d *(1 mark)*

2 d *(1 mark)*

3 You would get 1 mark for choosing an appropriate example; then you need to make three points in your explanation, for example:

- Young people seek to be like them/act like them in a positive way/and therefore want to participate in that particular activity.
- The fame/financial gain associated with that activity/encourages more young people to take it up.
- The profile of the activity is raised/within the media in particular/this can encourage greater

levels of sponsorship/spectators/participant performers. *(4 marks)*

28. Health and safety (page 75)

1 d *(1 mark)*

2 c *(1 mark)*

3 Your answer should make two developed points, for example:

- Because it is within the rules or laws of an activity and failing to do so could result in being booked or even sent off/banned from taking part.
- This is not within the spirit of the game.
- Because it can be dangerous to yourself/others if the techniques or action is wrong and can often result in an injury, sometimes serious ones/it clearly can affect safety. *(4 marks)*

29. Rules relating to sport and equipment (page 77)

1 d *(1 mark)*

2 a *(1 mark)*

3 You need to make two developed points to get the full 4 marks, for example:

- Football – if playing on a grass pitch, studded boots should be worn. This is to allow for a proper grip and to prevent players falling over or possibly sliding into other players when tackling.
- Trampoline – light gymnastic shoes should be worn/to prevent toes getting caught up in the webbing of the trampoline/or underneath the safety mats which surround the edges of the trampoline. *(4 marks)*

30. Science in sport (page 79)

1 d *(1 mark)*

2 c *(1 mark)*

3 An example answer: The use of graphite for tennis rackets has enabled the racket head to become larger. This does not add overall weight to the racket as it is a strong material. It also allows greater tension in the strings, which in turn allows the players to generate more power and so allows them to hit the ball harder and become a more effective player. *(4 marks)*

31. ICT in sport (page 81)

1 a *(1 mark)*

2 b *(1 mark)*

3 You would need to make two developed points or four short points. Some example answers are:

- It is designed to make competition fairer as decisions can be checked by the officials in charge.
- It allows players/performers to challenge decisions made if they feel the incorrect decision has been given, such as a ball not hitting the stumps in cricket or a ball landing on the line in tennis.

- The speed at which balls may be hit, or the action takes place, means that human error is possible. ICT technology allows for the correct decision to be made even if there is a slight delay in play.
- The technology has now been proven to be effective (football took a long time to decide to use goal-line technology as the authorities needed to be convinced that it worked). *(4 marks)*

Glossary

Abduction – the movement of a bone or limb away from the body

Accreditation – a formal official requirement which certifies your levels and qualifications

Adduction – the movement of a bone or limb towards the body

Agonist – the muscle that contracts to allow a movement to take place

Amateur – someone who takes part in sport, or an activity, as a pastime or hobby rather than for financial gain

Antagonist – the muscle that relaxes to allow a movement to take place

Apartheid – a policy of separating groups, especially because of race or colour

Arousal – the state of readiness of a performer

Carbo-load – eating foods that are high in starch to increase carbohydrate reserves in muscles

Cardiovascular system – the circulatory and respiratory systems working together; i.e. the circulation of blood and the transportation of oxygen and nutrients to the cells of the body and the waste products away from these cells

Culture – the ideas, customs and social behaviour of a particular people or society

Dehydration – the loss of water from the body

Ethnic – relating to a group of people with a common national or cultural tradition

Etiquette – the unwritten rules or conventions of any activity

Exercise – activity that requires physical or mental exertion, especially when performed to develop or maintain fitness

Extension – when the angle between two bones is increased

Extra-curricular activity – an activity that takes place out of timetabled lessons, such as pre-school, at lunchtime or after school

Extrinsic reward – something done for a particular reward which is clearly visible to others and which can be seen as an achievement

Flexion – when the angle between two bones is decreased

Heart rate – the number of times the heart beats in one minute. For the average resting adult the heart rate is approximately 72 beats per minute

High protein diet – a diet made up of a lot of protein and a reduced intake of carbohydrates and fats. Has been linked to kidney problems

Intrinsic reward – something that gives an individual an internal satisfaction achieved from doing something well

Joint – a connection point between two bones where movement occurs

Ligaments – bands of fibres that are attached to the bones and link the joints together

Metabolism – the biochemical processes that happen in the body and keep us alive

Motivation – your drive to succeed and desire and energy to achieve something

Muscle tone – the tension which remains in a muscle, even when at rest

Nimble – quick and light in movement; able to move with ease and rapidly

Overload – making your body work harder than normal in order to make it adapt or improve

Peers – people who are the same age and status as you

Physiological factor – one that affects your living body and therefore affects you physically

Plateauing – progressing to a certain level then seeming to get stuck there before being able to move on

Professional – someone who takes part in sport, or an activity, as a means of earning their livelihood. They are paid to do it as a full-time job

Progression – gradually and safely increasing the amount of training that you do

Progressive overload – where additional demands are added only gradually and safely

Pulse rate – the rate per minute at which the heart beats which can be located and measured at certain points in the body

Reversibility – the loss of positive effects if you stop training

Sedentary – sitting down or being physically inactive for long periods of time

Seeding – the best players or teams are chosen/selected to automatically qualify and be kept apart in early rounds

Somatotype – body type (endomorph, mesomorph or ectomorph)

Specificity – the particular kind of activity or exercise you use to build up or improve certain body systems or skills

Sprain – the overstretching or tearing of ligaments at a joint

Strain – the overstretching of a muscle

Strength – the maximum force that can be developed within a muscle or group of muscles during a single maximal contraction

Suppleness – when your muscles and joints work together so well that you can achieve the maximum range of movement without any pain or injury

Tendons – very strong cords that join the muscle to the bone